THE UNVEILING OF LOVE

THE UNVEILING OF LOVE

Sufism and the Remembrance of God

Sheikh Muzaffer Ozak

Translated from the Turkish
by Muhtar Holland

PIR PRESS ::: NEW YORK

"To Nur Lex Hixon
for all American lovers"

Pir Press
227 West Broadway
New York, New York 10013
pirpress@mindspring.com

First Pir Press Edition, 2001

Library of Congress Cataloging-in-Publication Data

Ozak, Muzaffer. 1916–1985
The Unveiling of Love.
1. Sufism. I. Title.
BP189.2.09713 297'.4 81-541
ISBN 1-879708-15-9

Printed and bound in the United States of America
Cover design: Peter Muller
Cover calligraphy: The seal of Sultan Muhammad Nureddin al-Jerrahi al-Halveti, founder of the Halveti Jerrahi Order

CONTENTS

A SHORT AUTOBIOGRAPHY

It was in 1916 (A.H. 1332) that my mother, Hajja Aysha Ozak, brought me into the world. My birthplace was our house near the tekke (Sufi meeting place) of the Jerrahi Dervishes in the Karagumruk quarter of Istanbul.

My father, Hajji Mehmed Efendi of Konya, was an Islamic scholar and a teacher at the court of Sultan Abdul Hamid. He was the first scholar in a long line of warriors. My two uncles were standard-bearers with the forces of Ghazi Osman Pasha, the hero of Plevna. One of them was promoted to the rank of general for his bravery in saving the standard from falling into the hands of the enemy. He was wounded in a later battle and taken prisoner by the Russians, but after his release from captivity he continued to serve as a general in the Ottoman army until the day he died. My other uncle, Bekir, fell in action at Plevna and was accorded a martyr's funeral.

My father's family was an old one, which divided into two branches: the Jebejioghullari and the Bashaghaoghullari. Breaking with the family's military tradition, my father Mehmed Efendi studied at the Kurshunlu *medrese* (Islamic school) in Suleymaniye, Istanbul. He was then posted to the school in Plevna, at that time still part of the Ottoman Empire, where he married my mother, Aysha Hanim.

My mother was the granddaughter of Seyyid Hussein Efendi, the Halveti Sheikh of the town of Yanbolu. Her father was Captain Ibrahim Agha, from the district of Eregli on the Black Sea, who had studied at the maritime college in the time of Sultan Mahmud the Just. Having fallen ill on a voyage to what is now Bulgaria, he went to seek treatment at the Yanbolu *tekke*. This was how my grandfather came to meet Sheikh Hussein Efendi, eventually joining his *tekke* through marriage to his daughter. Seyyid Hussein Efendi was brother to the governor of Yanbolu.

When the Balkan provinces were lost in 1878 (A.H. 1293), the surviving members of my family migrated to Istanbul, where my father received his appointment to the Imperial Palace. My father's ancestors belonged to the Kizilkecheli clan of the tribe known as Kayi Turk. My mother's family, the Ozaks, were Seyyids descended from 'Ali, son-in-law of the Prophet, on him be peace.

My father, Mehmed Efendi, died tragically when I was only six months old. My elder brother, Murad Reis, survived the 1914–1918 war, which caused the loss of many of my relatives, only to be killed one Friday in Istanbul by the Occupation forces. I had no one left but my mother, my sister, and two cousins, little girls orphaned by the war. We were destitute.

At that time, when I was five or six years old, I was taken into the care of my father's schoolmate, Seyyid Sheikh Abdurrahman Samiyyi Saruhani of the Kadiri, Naqshbandi, Ushaki, and Halveti orders, who saw to my upbringing for twelve years. During this time I finished primary school and was in the second year of secondary school when God took to His mercy my beloved Sheikh, who was as dear to me as my own father. Meanwhile I had been studying the Koran and had committed many parts of it to memory. I completed these studies under the chief Imam of the Fatih Mosque, Mehmed Rasim Efendi. For the next eight years I followed the lectures of Arnavut Husrev Efendi on Hadith and Islamic law. Poverty obliged me to work by day, but in the evenings I studied under Gumuljineli Mustafa Efendi, who was nicknamed the "Walking Library."

In due course I qualified as a muezzin and served in that capacity first at the Ali Yaziji, then at the Soghan Agha Mosque. From there I moved to the Kefeli Mosque in Karagumruk, where I was instructed by the Imam, Shakir Efendi, in the art of book dealing. Then I was appointed muezzin to the Grand Mosque of Beyazit, beside which the booksellers have their market.

It was while I was serving at this mosque that I met the Imam of Bakirkoy, Hafiz Ismail Hakki Efendi, who admired my voice and my style. This pupil of Eyuplu Hafiz Ahmed, the son of the famous musician Zekai Efendi of the Mevlevi Order, was to teach me the religious hymns and odes known as *ilahi, kaside, durak, mevlud,* and *mersiye.* My teacher was so fond of me that he gave to me in marriage his close relative Gulsum Hanum, who was headmistress of a school. Thus I became part of his family. I moved into my bride's house, near the Suleymaniye Mosque built by the famous architect Sinan. I had been appointed Imam of the Veznejiler Mosque, and for twenty-three years I was to serve as honorary Imam at the great Suleymaniye during the month of Ramadan. When my own mosque collapsed, I was appointed Imam of the mosque in the Covered Bazaar.

As this mosque had no pulpit, and was therefore unsuitable for Friday congregational prayers, the community helped to restore a nearby ruin and I started leading Friday prayers there, in response to popular demand. This restored mosque is known as Jamili Han. Although now retired from the Imamate, I still lead Friday prayers there and give guidance and instruction in an honorary capacity.

At present I am the owner of a large bookstore, which is visited by people from all over the world. I can claim some knowledge of old manuscripts, since before my military service I studied calligraphy and decorative art under the Chief Calligraphers at the Academy of Fine Art, Hajji Kamil, Hajji Nureddin, and Turakesh Ismail Hakki Bey, as well as having forty-two years of practical experience in the book trade.

My first marriage lasted twenty years, but produced no children. I remarried after the death of my first wife, and am now the father of a girl and a boy.

I have performed the Pilgrimage to Mecca and Medina eleven times. Iraq I have visited six times, Syria and Palestine eight, Egypt three. In all these places I got to know many Sufis and Sheikhs. I have also met Sheikhs and scholars in Istanbul and other Turkish cities, have enjoyed their company, and have learned their views and teachings.

But of all the venerable persons I have met, I profited most from the one who was my benefactor and first Sheikh of my tender years, Sheikh Samiyyi Saruhani Ushshakiyul-Halveti. This holy person wrote over twenty books on Islamic law and Sufism, in Turkish and in Arabic. All of these works have been published. I also know of his many unpublished manuscripts on chemistry, alchemy, herbal medicine, and other subjects, which were destroyed during a fire that wiped out a great part of Istanbul. In fact, he himself destroyed some of his books on chemistry and alchemy, being in doubt whether they would be used for good purposes. This wonderful person, with whom I spent much of my childhood, was loved and respected by all for his noble character, good humor, generosity, courage, friendliness, and humility.

The next guide I was to encounter during my early youth was another Halveti Sheikh from the Shabaniya branch, Seyyid Sheikh Ahmed Tahir ul-Marashi. His specialization was Sheikh ibn al-'Arabi. With him I studied *al-Futuhat al-Makkiya* and the *Fusus.* I studied the interpretation of the Koran under Nevshehirli Hajji Hayrullah and Atif Hoja. I followed the teachings of Hajji Abdul Hakim Arvasi and Sheikh Shefik Efendi, and with the wisdom received from these wonderful men of knowledge I have for thirty years preached to and taught the people in forty-two mosques in Istanbul, including huge crowds in the grand mosques of Sultan Ahmed (Blue Mosque), Yeni Jami, Nuruosmaniye, Beyazit, Laleli, Valide Sultan, Fatih, Eyub, Kojamustafa Pasha, and Suleymaniye.

During my early youth, while studying Koran interpretation at the Aya Sofya Mosque in Istanbul, I dreamed one night of the Prophet, on him be peace. He was riding his camel, led by Imam 'Ali, may God be pleased with him, who was holding in his other hand his famous sword, the two-edged Zulfikar. Addressing me, the Prophet asked if I had faith and if I was a Muslim. When I said yes, he asked me if I would give my head for Islam. Again I said yes. Then the Prophet told Imam 'Ali to cut my head off in the name of Islam. Imam 'Ali asked me to stretch my neck out, then struck me with all his might, severing my head from my body. I awoke in terror. When I saw my Koran teacher next morning, I told him my dream and then told him who my father was. I knew he was a close friend of my late father, but I had never mentioned it before. He shook his head and said: "Ah, so you are the son of my fellow exile, are you?" My father and my teacher were among the seven hundred Sheikhs and theologians who were banished to the port of Sinop on the Black Sea by the revolutionaries of the Committee of Union and Progress, for having supported the Sultan. The exile of these religious dignitaries had continued until the First World War in 1914.

My teacher then interpreted my dream and said that I was going to join the Sufi path of 'Ali and that I would become the Sheikh of a particular order.

Many years after that incident, when I had opened my store of rare books near the Beyazit Mosque and become a well-known Imam and preacher, I had another dream. I was in the middle of the Bosphorus between the Topkapi Palace and Uskudar, in a small sailing boat whose sails were torn and whose mast was broken. A terrible storm was raging. Someone handed me a sheet of paper and told me to read it so that I would be saved from the calamity. When I came back to my shop next morning, I saw the very person who had given me the paper in my dream, passing in front of my shop. I could not gather the courage to call him. A couple of days later I dreamed about the same person. He was walking on the other side of the street and beckoned to me with his walking stick. The next morning, in amazement, I again saw him passing in front of my shop. I felt that there was a spiritual meaning to these dreams, but I did nothing about it. A short while later I saw the same man again in a dream in which he hugged me so hard that I felt my bones about to break. Then he let me go, held up the crown of the Halveti Order, and put the turban on my head. I felt crushed under the weight of the turban. It was as if the seven heavens were sitting on my head.

As soon as I came to open my shop in the morning, I saw the man walking by, stick in hand. I told myself: "There is a mystery and a spiritual message in this situation. I am not going to call this man. Let him come to me." He walked by, my eyes following him, then he stopped and came and stood in front of my shop, stuck his head through the door, and said: "You bigot, three times you have seen me. When are you going to start having faith?"

"Right now," said I, grabbing and kissing his hand. This holy person was Seyyid Sheikh Ahmed Tahir ul-Marashi, the Sheikh of the Halveti-Shabani. I became his dervish, and he would come to my shop every day. Some days he would speak, on others remain silent, but in either case he would be teaching me. This continued for seven years.

During this time I met a friend of my master, Evranoszade Sami Bey, who belonged to the same order. It was he who clad me in the dervish cloak. In that ceremony, I knew so little that I objected to the cloak being put on my shoulders: "O Master, how can I permit someone like you to hold my cloak for me?" I was told that my mind did not yet grasp the subtle meaning, but that they were giving me the dervish cloak to wear.

Sami Bey left this world one Night of Power. Three years later my master Tahir Efendi fell and broke his hip as he was walking from my shop. As I was trying to lift him up, he said: "They have been trying to destroy me, and now at last they have succeeded." He lasted three months. When I visited him before his death, he once showed me the crown of the saint Ibrahim Kushadali and said, "If I go, let Mustafa Efendi keep this crown." This Mustafa Efendi was one of his *khalifas.* Then one day my master called me and told me his last wishes. He died the next day, which was a Saturday, and we buried him in the graveyard of the Fatih Mosque, next to Sheikh Turbedar Efendi, who had been his Sheikh.

That night, having submitted to God the question whether I should become the dervish of Mustafa Efendi, I dreamed that he was laughing at me boisterously. I could not ascribe a meaning to this, so I submitted my question a second time. That night I dreamed that he was shouting at me angrily and calling me "softy." Under these circumstances I could not become his dervish. I was left for a while without a Sheikh, waiting for a spiritual message. During that time I visited the *tekke* of the Kadiris in Beyoglu and then the Rifais in Kasim Pasha. The Halveti *tekke* had burned down. These two places were the only centers where the dhikr ceremony was held.

During that time Gavsi Efendi, the Sheikh of the Kadiris, tried to persuade me to become his *khalifa,* using as intermediaries Ismail Efendi, the Sheikh of the Bedevis; Jevat Efendi, the Sheikh of the Sadis; and Colonel Salahettin Efendi, the Sheikh of the Sunbulis. I told them that although my Sheikh was dead, I was a Halveti; thus I could not decide by myself, but would have to submit the matter and wait for a spiritual message; if I received a positive answer, I would not need to be a *khalifa,* but would gratefully accept to be a humble dervish of the Sheikh.

Sheikh Gavsi Efendi kept pressing me, and finally insisted that I should come to the *dergah* (Sufi meeting place) unshaven the next

Friday, which was the holy day of Ragha'ib, the first Friday of the month of Rajab.

That night I submitted my problem and dreamed that I was performing dhikr at the *tekke* of the Halveti-Jerrahis in Karagumruk, bareheaded, barefoot, and half-naked, while the Sheikh, Seyyid Fahri Efendi, was sitting by the window, in an ordinary suit but wearing a white prayer cap. He was singing the eulogy by Sheikh Galip: "Your sermon is read from the pulpit of eternity; your verdict is given in the court of Judgment Day; your chant of praise is sung on earth and in Heaven. You are my beloved Ahmad, Mahmud, Muhammad."

I woke up. Everything was clear. But how was I to present myself to Fahri Efendi? As far as I knew his *tekke* was closed. I had known him slightly, when I used to take Hadith lessons from Mustafa Efendi, the "Walking Library." He used to take me by the hand to see the Sheikh, complaining to him that I had become too rigidly dogmatic, then make me kiss his hand and ask him to pray for me. But so many years had passed. Perhaps I had seen him a few times at his house during Ramadan, when we were invited to break the fast. I was merely a child at that time. Since then I had become a preacher of some repute. I had a lot of followers. As the *tekkes* were officially closed, the Sufis gathered clandestinely. I did not even know whether he was still teaching and had followers. Nevertheless I decided to go to his house late one night after the night prayer, telling myself that the Sheikhs are gracious and that he would not turn me away from his door.

The door was opened by a young dervish, to whom I introduced myself, asking permission to see the Sheikh. I was invited into a small room where I saw the master with three other men. He paid me the honor of standing to receive me, and asked me to take a seat. I was ready to abstain from my usual cigarette, but he offered me one and said smilingly: "Don't be embarrassed. Smoke, and have a cup of coffee too. Coffee without a cigarette is like sleeping without a blanket in winter." He added: "Among ourselves we attach more importance to love than to respect." When he asked me the reason for my visit, I told him what was going on between me and the Kadiri Sheikh Gavsi Efendi, and about the result of my meditation and the dream. Then I told him who I was, where I was born, who my father was. He laughed and said: "Who doesn't know the famous preacher to women?"

I responded: "If I could find some men, I would preach to them too."

In religion, of course, there is no fundamental difference between men and women. I was in fact preaching to both sexes, but I understood the point he was making: *Real* men would not be prevented from remembering and calling upon God at every moment. Then he told me: "Indeed your dream points to us, but let me also submit the matter and see what message I receive." He asked me to come back on Monday. Then I took my leave.

That Monday, Sefer Efendi, who was a young dervish then and who is now my *khalifa,* brought a letter delaying my meeting with the Sheikh to the following Friday. That Friday, having received a positive message from the Unseen, Sheikh Fahri Efendi accepted me as his dervish. Thus I preferred to become a dervish of the Halveti-Jerrahis rather than a *khalifa* of the Kadiris. I followed my duties as a dervish to the last detail, and visited my Sheikh two or three times a week. A happy man with a great sense of humor, he was brave, intelligent, and prudent. He was a master of dream interpretation, a faculty given especially to the Halveti Order. He was a man whose conversation was a delight, whose miracles were well known. Loved and respected by everyone, he was a man who made us taste the love of the Prophet, the mysteries of the saints; a compassionate man and a generous one who protected the poor and bound everyone to himself.

Sometimes he used to joke with me so much that he pushed me to the verge of anger, hoping to get a reaction from me. Then he would publicly declare that I was invited by our Saint Nureddin Jerrahi and no one could touch me. Later I was told that the master had often mentioned my name six months before my coming to the *tekke*. Six months after my becoming a Jerrahi dervish, I dreamed that three men came to examine me. From the questions and answers I clearly felt that two of them wanted me to pass this test and one of them did not. This was an examination to qualify as an Imam. I was able to convince the third man that I was an Imam already, and was therefore accepted by unanimous vote.

Although I knew that dreams should be told immediately, I could not do so the next day because I was too busy. That night, I went to sleep after praying for three or four hours, and dreamed an extremely ugly and shameful dream. When I woke up, I was revolted with myself and said to myself: "That is your reward for praying three or four hours." Somehow I was not able to see my Sheikh that day either, and even if I had seen him, how could I have told him the shameful dream?

The third night I dreamed that I went to the tekke and saw the dervishes praying in a very strange way, not reciting correctly and not doing the movements properly. I passed through in astonishment and met my Sheikh in the garden. He caught me by one ear and lifted me off the ground. With his other hand he kept slapping my left side as if he were dusting a rug. Then he pulled me into a room which was full of garbage. He said: "Clean this room, it is going to be yours." Later I saw that the room of which I had dreamed was the room of the head *khalifa*.

When I woke up, I knew that this was my punishment for not telling my dream to my master. I rushed to his house and told him the first and last dreams, leaving out the shameful one. He smiled and told me: "You could not have had those two dreams without a shameful one in the middle." I begged to be left alone with him to tell him the ugly dream. When I told him, he declared me his *khalifa*.

For nine years we stayed very close together. One year before he died, he became ill in the middle of the dhikr and put me in charge. I led the dhikr that whole year while he was sick. At the end of that year, on the 5th of Shaban, which is the day of the martyrdom of Imam Hasan, a Wednesday night at ten minutes to ten, he went to the eternal abode, to the gardens of high heaven, and received the gift of being close to the Messenger of God. The next day, in accordance with his last wishes, I gave him the ritual ablution, while Sefer Baba and Kemal Baba poured the water. On Friday I led his funeral prayers at the Fatih Mosque. Followed by thousands of lovers we brought his coffin on our shoulders to his room in the *tekke*, which he had built seven years before his death, and buried him close to our Saint Nureddin Jerrahi. The prayers at his tomb were recited by the famous Shemseddin Yeshil Efendi. Acting upon another dream I had dreamed, and although the activities of the Sufis were forbidden and the *tekkes* were closed by law, the very day after his departure I opened the doors of the *tekke* to the public, to friends and enemies alike.

Having occupied the sheepskin throne of our Saint Nureddin Jerrahi for fifteen years now, I humbly continue teaching my Turkish dervishes, as well as many lovers of truth from all parts of the world.

I am the nineteenth Sheikh and eighth *khalifa* since the creation of our branch of the order. With the strength received from the will of God, the wish of His Messenger, the good pleasure of my Saint, the spirituality of all the Sheikhs before me, and the blessing and faith of my master and benefactor, I look forward to being involved in the spiritual guidance of lovers till the day I die. I have only two children born of my blood, but God knows the number of my spiritual children. I have had the honor of seeing the Prophet, on him be peace, seventeen times in the world of dreams. I have seen Moses, Jesus, John, and Khidr once. I have seen both the venerable Abu Bakr and ‘Umar twice, and in one of these dreams I kissed their hands. I have seen both our lady Fatima and Imam 'Ali twice, and Imam Hasan and Imam Hussein once. I have seen my Saint Nureddin Jerrahi twice, receiving his compliments.

I have traveled to Germany six times, twice to England, and twice to Holland and Belgium, and have seen Paris four times. I have met many good and interesting people during these travels. I have also visited Rumania, Bulgaria, Yugoslavia, and Greece. I have been to America four times, where my dervishes and I performed the dhikr and held talks in many cities.

Only God knows what will happen next. I pray that the love of lovers may increase from day to day. Success comes only from God.

FOREWORD

The author of *The Unveiling of Love* is my revered master, teacher, and guide along the way to Truth, Sheikh Muzaffer Ozak al-Jerrahi al-Halveti. May God Almighty grant him long life, to be a blessing for all seekers of truth.

Of the nine books my Sheikh has written in Turkish, works that contain the essence of his spiritual teaching over nearly forty years, *The Unveiling of Love* is the first to appear in English translation. It is a comparatively short work, written for the benefit of the Americans he loves so much for their "crystal-clear hearts and still clearer eyes-of-the-heart." The purpose of the book is to point out the path of Love—the way of the Sufi—and invite the reader to embark upon it. This path is shown to be the surest and the straightest way from "the lowest of the low" to "the fairest form"* in creation—the Human Being.

The whole emotional content of *The Unveiling of Love* is the experienced wisdom of the Holy Book, the Prophets, on them be God's blessing and peace, and the Sufi sages, God's pleasure be on

*Koran 95 (al-Tin): 4–5

them. The language is traditional in style, yet addresses itself unmistakably to the understanding of the "clear hearts" of the American lovers.

We all have hearts able to love, but the heart remains dormant until the magic kiss of Prince Charming, the object of love, wakes us up. Even for the seeker of the love of God and of Truth, the object of love is hidden, veiled, invisible. It is not because it does not exist that we do not see it, but because we are asleep and our eyes are closed. Either we shall stay asleep and dream our life away, waking up only when we die and meeting Reality with the horror of meeting the unaccustomed; or we shall be awakened by the loving kiss of a sage and find faith, love, hope, and life eternal.

May this book help the sincere reader so that the veil may be lifted from the beautiful face of the Beloved.

A servant at my master's door,

Tosun Bayrak al-Jerrahi al-Halveti
Jerrahi Order of America

AUTHOR'S PREFACE

In the name of God, All-Merciful and Compassionate.

All praise and glory belongs to God, the Lord of Majesty and Perfection. "We have indeed honored the children of Adam" is the mystery He reveals to us, His unworthy servants. For He created us "in fairest form," in token of His everlasting mercy, love, kindness, and generosity. Our Lord adorned the heart of Adam with all His names and with remembrance of Him. He adorned with His very Essence the heart of His beloved Muhammad Mustafa, on him be God's blessing and peace. By sending him as His mercy to all beings, God honored the sons of Adam with the Light of Muhammad, on him be peace, and with His own manifestation. Thus we see nothing but Him and sing nothing but His sacred names.

Grateful blessings and perfect salutations to the beloved and intimate friend of Allah, the One God without partner or peer—to Muhammad, on him be peace, the healing remedy of the distressed; owner of the station of *Mahmud* on the day of Resurrection; mercy to all worlds; the *Ahmad* of heavenly scripture; *Muhammad* of all time, past and future; *Hamid*, the reason for all existence, to whom it was said, "I have created all for you, and you for Myself." As our Lord, Exalted and Glorified is He, informs us in His Noble Koran,

His Endless Being and all His angels send blessings eternally to the light of His Essence, to the mirror of Truth, to the beauty of His attributes which is His beloved Messenger, and He commands all His faithful servants to do the same.

Abundant blessings and salutations also to his descendants, his family, his companions, and his intimate friends, and to the sages who follow his path of light, each of them a guiding star for us. We humble servants have received the good news that whoever among us follows one of these blessed beings will find God's pleasure, approval, grace, and P aradise.

In the beginning of February 1978, I went to Germany with twenty-two of my disciples after being invited to perform at the Traditional Art Festival in Berlin. We conducted the noble Halveti-Jerrahi ceremony in the city's enormous opera house. As is customary, the ceremonies of the Friends of God are adorned with Turkish Sufi music. In the course of our performance we sang the mystic hymns of some of the great Sufi masters including Yunus Emre, Hajji Bayram Veli and Eshrefoglu Rumi. We were received with great interest and love.

The opera house, with a capacity of fifteen hundred people, was completely filled. I learned later from the organizers that many had to remain outside. Among this large crowd there were quite a few famous personalities from all over Europe with more or less knowledge concerning Sufi orders.

As usual, the noble ceremony started with the *Tawhid,* or the declaration of Divine Unity. It is worth mentioning that many of those present chanted with us the words of the *Tawhid,* which are LA ILAHA ILLA-LLAH. Others sat in grave silence and followed with such intent that it seemed as if they didn't dare to take a breath.

After chanting the *Tawhid,* we rose to our feet to form the circle of Unity. I could perceive the amazement and immense excitement of the people who joined us in the ceremony. This enormous crowd appeared to be thirsty for the *Tawhid* and eager to quench their thirst by taking part in our ceremony.

Almost all European universities have professors who specialize in the literature and philosophy of Sufism. Scholars within these learning institutions are constantly researching and preparing studies in Islamic, and particularly Turkish, Sufism, as well as the esoteric movements of other religions. These academics compare religious traditions and impart their vast and detailed knowledge to large numbers of students. In Europe, therefore, one can find very learned experts in various esoteric studies, including Sufism.

Although both educators and students have deepened their theoretical knowledge of these mystical traditions, often they have never seen them in practice. In our gathering we were able to show them the reality of what they had only previously known through books and academic studies. They were fascinated to see with their own eyes what they had studied in the abstract, and were clearly enraptured with our presentation. The mystic hymns penetrated the hearts of those in this great gathering. The noble Circle in which the dervishes participated in ecstasy also brought the audience to ecstasy.

During the ceremony of Divine Remembrance and recital of the *Tawhid*, many of the fifteen hundred people joined in the chanting with love and enjoyment, so that the opera house resonated with the cries of ALLAH and HU. We were truly beholding a magnificent sight. As the Divine Remembrance and our noble ceremony came to an end, the crowd boiled over with enthusiasm and excitement. With the call of ALLAHU AKBAR, the flood of applause was cut short.

After giving our greetings of peace to all those present and withdrawing with my dervishes, the people, thinking that we were just pausing, stayed in their seats. After it was announced a few times that the ceremony was finished, the audience finally understood. Suddenly, many members of the audience came in groups to the room where we had gone. They congratulated us each individually and let us know their great appreciation.

At that moment it seemed to me that this large crowd was colored with the light of *Tawhid* and was gathered in Unity. This enormous interest and love made me think that the Christian Church in the West had been deficient in its capacity to satisfy the spiritual longing of the people of Europe. But the spiritual feelings evoked in those present by the noble circle of the Friends of God and their practice of Unity did bring them satisfaction. In this state of ecstasy, Truth enraptured them and brought them closer to the understanding of Divine Reality.

After we rested for a day we headed for Paris, and from there we went to the city of Rennes where another festival of traditional art was taking place. It is said that the city of Rennes was the capital of Christianity in France. The mayor of the city received us in City Hall, welcomed us with friendly greetings, and congratulated us and the other groups that were participating in the festival. After a short talk, a banquet was given for all the groups from other nations. We stayed three days and nights in Rennes.

Just as in Germany, the people who attended our performance at the appointed arena participated in the ceremony of Remembrance with enthusiasm. We rested during the day and spent the nights in the Remembrance of God. I can say with complete ease, since there is no reason for praising my humble self, that people who were carried away by the light of Divine Remembrance and the profession of Divine Unity, experienced ecstasy with increasing love and desire each time they participated in the noble ceremony with us.

When our ritual was completed, those who gathered around us began asking questions concerning Sufism and the profession of Divine Unity. Of course, it did not escape our attention that some tried to test us, while taking pains not to show their intention. But one thing was surely certain: without regard to either ideology or nationality, there was a great desire and zeal to call out "Allah."

One night I encountered the following question: "Although you are Muslims, you accept Christians without any discrimination into your ceremony and allow them to participate in the Remembrance of Divine Unity. Can you explain the wisdom behind this?"

I gave the following answer: "I am a humble Muslim and a spiritual guide. I accept anyone who utters 'Allah' in my ceremony. I call out to 'Allah' and I make people call out to 'Allah.'" I guess this answer satisfied the questioner.

It remains to be said that the duty of all prophets is to make people affirm LA ILAHA ILLA-LLAH, the profession of Divine Unity, regardless of their nationality, color or race. Thus we, being the inheritors of the prophets—thank God—have the duty first of all to encourage those we encounter to profess the Divine Unity.

I found explaining this useful, since I witnessed and validated for myself that, whether in Paris or in Rennes, people were truly thirsting for the experience of Divine Unity and Remembrance. Let me also add that in both places magazines and newspapers published articles praising us.

An instance of this was in *Dunya,* an Istanbul newspaper, which published an article with a photograph of the dhikr ceremony. Quoting French publications, the article bore the heading: "Our Dervishes Have Enchanted the Europeans."

> The Turkish group of dervishes that participated in the traditional art festival in the city of Rennes attracted much interest. Their performances, accompanied by Sufi music, were more popular than those by French performers or groups from other countries. The French press singled out the Turkish dervishes especially for praise. Twenty-five music and dance groups participated. More than fifteen thousand spectators attended the festival this year, as compared to twelve thousand last year. One correspondent commented on the performances of the groups participating in the name of Turkey as follows:

> The dervishes presented the most splendid performances of Turkish spiritual music. It was impossible to not be impressed and amazed, especially by the way they implored God in prostration, their palms striking the floor in unison, and by their turning and whirling in ecstasy, which made the spectators hair stand on end. These humble dervishes were definitely one of the groups that drew the most attention.

I don't see any necessity in keeping a secret of how much I and those of like mind were moved as we listened to what was said and written about us in the European newspapers and magazines. We were touched by their articles expressing such great interest in us and so full of praise and affection. Actually, it was not our talents that made us shine in front of the Europeans; it was the divine light of Unity and the Remembrance of God. It is obvious that the light that dazzled the eyes of the people that came to see the music and dance from 25 countries was the light of the Divine that shone through our sacred Remembrance.

Indeed, I have to emphasize again that the Europeans we encountered were thirsting for the experience of Divine Unity. Even though they did not understand the meaning and spiritual subtleties of the hymns, they were affected by the rhythm and harmony of the incomparable ceremonial music. This encounter would certainly leave a lasting impression in their hearts. I wonder what spiritual state they would have come to if they had understood the meaning of the songs and the words that we chanted; if they could have understood, for example, the eloquent and concise expressions in the noble saint Yunus Emre's ecstatic hymns. What is certain is that the profession of Divine Unity had enchanted them, and that the odes of the sublime friends of God had made them drunk and bewildered. It seemed as if people had forgotten their personal identities, cultures and religions, and had transcended themselves. They mixed among the dervishes, participated in the Turning, and united with us in love and joy.

However, since this is not a memoir of my travels, it is not necessary to convey my other observations at length. In the future, I hope to write about impressions of my travels in detail, if the years left to me suffice.

We left the French people of Rennes and Paris, who had embraced us in their hearts with hospitality and inner sincerity, like a body leaving its soul. By divine permission and at the invitation of some Americans, we stepped into the New World after an eight hour flight.

I was met with great warmth and sincerity by those American lovers whom I had previously had the good pleasure to meet when they had traveled to Istanbul especially to grace me with their visit, and with whom I was close friends from then on; and by those who had learned of my name, but whom I had not yet had the chance to meet. After the usual welcome and ceremonies of introduction, our American friends got our luggage, divided us up into different cars, and brought us to the house of Professor Tosun Bayrak, where we were to stay as guests.

My friends in New York told me of a radio talk show on Sunday mornings devoted to the subject of religion and spirituality. They suggested that I agree to be interviewed on this program. Understanding this as a divine gift, I accepted. The moderator, who was introduced to me as Lex Hixon, initiated a discussion on the profession of Divine Unity and Divine Remembrance with Professor Tosun Bayrak, who is truly knowledgeable concerning religion and, especially, Sufi terminology. As I placed my total trust in Professor Tosun—although first, of course, in God—I was sure that he translated what I said exactly by the letter, and so had total peace of mind.

We began the program with the call to prayer, followed by some recitations of the Noble Koran. After I explained the meaning of the Arabic words and the interpretation of the Koranic verses just recited, I came to the subject of Divine Remembrance and Divine Unity.

Suddenly, Lex Hixon interrupted my talk:

"Efendi, can you demonstrate dhikr for the American lovers, so we can hear it with your own voice?"

I repeated the profession of Divine Unity a few times, and then Lex Hixon was moved to make an interesting comment. Since the Arabic pronunciation might be hard for the American lovers, he asked whether I could recite this protective and noble expression slowly, syllable by syllable, so that it could be learned and repeated correctly. As I considered this request very appropriate, I recited slowly: LA-ILA-HA-ILL-AL-LAH. Thus it became easy to understand, learn and recite.

He then asked whether we could perform the dhikr with everyone in the studio and with all the people who were listening everywhere.

When I answered positively, he made the following announcement to our audience:

"O lovers listening to this discussion, please take your phones off the hook and shut your doors. We will now profess Divine Unity!"

I could not hold back my tears and began to cry. How I would have cried on, but millions of Americans were sitting by their radios and expecting me to perform the dhikr. I started to chant LA ILAHA ILLA-LLAH and all the American lovers there joined in. It seemed to me as if the American sky was filled with the *Tawhid* and the whole creation was listening. The earth and sky and whatever was between them, known or unknown, seen or unseen, everything was illuminated with the light of Divine Unity.

The Americans who were broadcasting in the radio station filled up our studio as the program went on. Later, people who listened to us from far away places, such as Canada, Washington, Alaska, California and Texas, as well as other states whose names I don't know, came to New York City in order to visit me. There was a young man named Hardy who astounded me by enduring a twenty-seven hour train ride in order to join the company of this humble servant of God.

During our sojourn in America, we demonstrated the rules of conduct of the Halveti-Jerrahi Order in the live performance of our ceremony. All the lovers and scholars who were researching and studying Sufi Orders participated in our performances with affection and joy. Before every performance Professor Talat Halman gave a talk about Sufism, explaining the meaning of these performances by giving understandable, fair and insightful explanations of Islamic mysticism.

We were offered the opportunity to perform the ceremony of Divine Remembrance in the great cathedral of St. John the Divine in New York City. Without hesitation I accepted. As we approached the Cathedral at dusk, we saw a large crowd waiting with anticipation. The dean of the Cathedral welcomed us respectfully and showed us to a place where we could rest and change into our ceremonial clothing.

After our initial greetings to and blessings upon the Prophet, we commenced the noble circle of the saints of Allah with the mystical hymns of our order and the chanting of the profession of Divine Unity. As states of ecstasy from this Remembrance of Unity manifested in the dervishes, the spectators suddenly seemed to be so impressed that they began chanting with us. People in the audience came forward, forming a second circle around us, and joined in the ceremony of Remembrance. With the cry of ILAHA ILLA-LLAH and ALLAH they threw themselves into the circle, engaging in the remembrance of Divine Unity with divine rapture.

The mystic chants echoed in the vast dome of the Cathedral, and truly ascended in waves to the Throne of the Merciful One. All those present were enveloped in Divine Love, and upon all, without exception, was cast the intoxication of Divine Unity. While we were engaged in Divine Remembrance I saw with my own eyes the Cathedral shaking and the paintings on the walls vibrating to such a degree that they appeared as if they were about to fall down.

During one of my talks with the American lovers, fruit was brought to eat. In order to joke with them a little, I asked the following question:

"How would you like me to share this fruit? Should I divide the fruit according to God's justice or by the justice of a servant of God?"

"We want God's justice!"

I divided the fruit among three people and did not give anything to the others. As they had waited with curiosity for the result of their request, I then gave them this explanation:

"This is indeed God's justice. He gives some of his servants a lot, and others are deprived."

Without thinking, they replied:

"If that is God's justice, we are satisfied with it."

Understanding that my Lord had graciously bestowed upon them the intimate knowledge of Divine Unity, my eyes filled with tears, and my heart expanded and found happiness.

At another gathering, I wanted to measure their degree of knowledge by means of a joke. I asked them:

"What is there that God can not see?"

Lex Hixon, to whom I had given the Sufi name of Nur, which means Divine Light, answered:

"There is nothing that God does not know or see. God, though, may choose not to see the sins of some of his beloved servants."

He meant that God may forgive the mistakes of his beloved servants.

That was not, however, what I had expected as an answer. The answer I had wanted was that God does not see dreams, because the Divine Essence does not get overwhelmed by the forgetfulness, sleep or absent-mindedness that makes dreaming possible. Although Lex's response was different from what I had expected, it increased my love for him.

From midnight until 3 AM we continued to talk about Divine Unity and Truth, and the Remembrance of God. When I reminded them of the time so that they could go to sleep and rest, they silenced me with the following objection:

"Don't you love us Efendi? Is that why you want us to sleep? We will soon fall into such a sleep that it will last until the Day of Judgment. Efendi, you will be with us for only a few more days. Wouldn't we gladly sacrifice sleep for more precious moments spent in your presence?"

When I rose after two hours of slumber for the early morning prayers, I swear by God I found a few of them repeating the profession of Divine Unity and praying with their rosaries.

The refined persons who came to me during this and my subsequent visits, asked many questions concerning Sufism, the profession of Divine Unity and the ceremony of Remembrance. They turned each and every one of our gatherings into a Garden of Paradise where Divine Mercy rained down in torrents.

Through close scrutiny of every one of these people, I have clear evidence that each of them was a lover of God Most High. Their hearts were as pure, clean and beautiful as their faces and their outer forms. Their moral qualities could be perceived in the beauty of their physical appearance. Without exception, they all asked for insight into the Real Beloved and strongly desired to converse with me about God and Love. May nobody understand or interpret this wrongly!

I must confess that the love for God that I witnessed in America, I have seen very little in the Middle Eastern countries that I have visited. With this statement, I believe I have fulfilled my duty of appreciation.

There was not one eye that did not shed tears, not one tongue that did not say "Allah," and not one heart that did not fill with the love of Truth as the ceremony of Divine Remembrance began. It seemed as if the profession of Divine Unity was constantly on their tongues. It did not even cross their minds to eat or drink. The air they were breathing, the water they were drinking, whatever sustained them was filled with the love of God. I do not exaggerate. They did not eat, drink or sleep. Instead, they were constantly talking and inquiring about God. Their love and passion for God made them forget their physical needs and transformed them almost into angels. All of them were as pure and innocent as children.

This humble book is an inspiration which came through them. I consider it a modest gift dedicated to, and in appreciation of, one of these American lovers, Nur Lex Hixon.

This unworthy beggar, full of sin and in need of the enlightenment of the Lord of Power, Muzaffer Ozak, who keeps the tomb and sits at the threshold of our Master, the Axis of the Sufis, Pir Nureddin Jerrahi, may God illuminate and sanctify his spirit, begs his dear readers' indulgence in overlooking any shortcomings or mistakes that may appear in this book. May God, Exalted is He, reward them for it.

My thanks and gratitude to all who helped to put together this humble work, especially to the Dia Art Foundation for their help; to al-Hajj Muhtar Holland, who translated my words into English as if I might have spoken them myself; to Professor al-Hajj Tezfik Topuzoglu and Sheikh Tosun Bayrak al-Jerrahi who helped in the translation; to Simon Bryquer, al-Hajja Reyhan Bray, and my other dervishes in America who helped edit, type, and correct the manuscript; as well as Ehud Sperling and Claudine Fischer, who showed extreme sensitivity and delicacy in the organization and publishing of the text, and to everyone involved in the work from the typesetter and the designer to the printer and the people who carried the paper and printed books.

I beseech the Lord of the Whole Universe that the hearts of those who helped in the preparation of this work and those who read *The Unveiling of Love* may be filled with the love of God and the affection of God and His Messenger, that they be blessed with the spiritual grace of the Intimates of God, and that every one of them may find his true goal and desire.

Success comes only from God, Exalted is He.

Keeper of the holy sanctuary of Pir Nureddin al-Jerrahi al-Halveti
Sheikh al-Hajji Ashki al-Jerrahi al-Halveti Muzaffer Ozak
Istanbul, April 9, 1978

THE ROOM IN THE HOUSE

1

AFFECTION

I was a hidden treasure. Then I wanted to make
Myself known, so I created creation.

Hadith Qudsi

Affection is the basis for the creation of the entire universe, all beings and creatures. Everything has affection as its base and foundation. Affection is the marrow and essence of all worlds, visible or invisible, known or unknown. Affection is the secret of creation. This truth is brought out and established quite plainly in the Sacred Tradition cited above. It is with affection, therefore, that I humbly wish to begin.

Affection means love and mutual loving. In Turkish, it is called *muhabbet,* derived from the Arabic root *hubb.* The word comes to mean the soul's inclination toward something, material or spiritual, in which it takes pleasure and delight; its various manifestations fall into three main sections:

1. A person is so fond of what he loves, and has such an affection for it, that his need for the object of his love comes to be as natural and necessary to him as air, water, and food. He cannot do without it, cannot live without it. Just as a human being cannot survive without breathing air, drinking water, and eating food, that individual cannot live without seeing the object of his affection, being together with it, and smelling its perfume. His life depends upon the object of his affection, and to its affection he owes his continuing survival.

In reality, it is for oneself that one has affection, it is oneself that one loves. Thus, it is because one sees one's own attributes and characteristics in the person for whom one has affection that one comes to love and have affection for that person. From one point of view, this affection is essentially an affection for one's own attributes and characteristics.

For instance, two people seize every opportunity to meet and get acquainted. They like the look of each other, so they become friends. As their temperaments and characters are dissimilar, however, they split up after a little while, feel an aversion for each other, and may even turn into enemies. This is because their outward appearances do not correspond to what they are like inside, and their dispositions and attitudes are incompatible.

2. A person seeks and asks after the one he is fond of only when he needs something. If he does not need anything in particular, he leaves meetings entirely to chance. This kind of affection can only be compared to the way you look for a washroom when you need to relieve yourself; having attended to the physiological necessity, you go on your way and do not look for the place again until another such need arises. Affection like this is obviously unacceptable in reason and logic. For it is not so much affection as interest that is the chief factor here, the object being to satisfy need and obtain benefit under the guise of affection. This cannot, therefore, be called affection for a friend; it can perhaps be explained as affection for the sake of personal profit and advantage.

It often happens this way in our practical everyday life. Somebody who hopes to get a job done, or a need attended to, approaches another with a show of friendship. If the person approached is disposed to kindness, though laughing up his sleeve at this display of artificial friendship, he will do what the sham friend wants him to do and see him off. The pretender, not realizing his own foolishness, supposes the person who just did his job for him to be a fool; in spite of the kindness shown to him, he thinks that he has cheated the other, whereas he really deceives himself.

If the person approached is not a kindly disposed individual, he does not want to let himself be exploited, so he will make up some lie to refuse the false friend's request. Or else he may promise to do what he can, laughing under his breath at making it sound credible, and then fail to keep his word.

3. As for the third and final type of affection, it is to avoid the lover as if fleeing from an infectious and contagious disease. When the lover wishes to approach the object of his liking, the loved one runs from him as if escaping an infectious and contagious disease and tries to get as far away from him as possible.

Whether openly or in secret, these three types of affection involve worldly benefits, beauty, rank and status, youth, health, life, and wealth. Although affection may appear to be for a friend, it is really affection for the benefits to be obtained.

Let us take for example the first type of material affection:

An affection of this apparently ideal kind is the culmination and perfection of material affection. As we have said, it is no more possible for one who loves with this kind of affection to live without the object of his love than it is for him to live without air, water, and food. As for the one loved with this sort of affection, it is that person's beauty, youth, or life that attracts the love and affection. For in affection of this kind there is no question of worldly advantage, rank and status, or wealth. These are peculiarly confined to the second type of affection. Very well, then, but now I ask:

Will you be able to love that person, whom you cannot do without and cannot live without, with the same affection when he or she has aged and grown physically ugly? Youth, beauty, even life itself, are things that no one can keep forever. Will you be able to feel the same affection when the one you love in health and good spirits has fallen ill? When your dear one has died, will you be able to go on loving as in life?

There is only one answer that can be given to these questions: No!

In other words, material love and affection are based only on particular advantages; when the advantage disappears, the love and affection also vanish.

And so?

And so the essential thing is to discover true affection.

2

TRUE AFFECTION

As for the affection desired by God, Exalted is He, it is the affection that never ceases for any cause or reason and that sustains itself without consideration of reward and benefit.

This affection is called *hubb fi-allah,* love for the sake of God. One who loves for God's sake goes on loving even when beauty turns to ugliness, youth turns to age, health changes to sickness, and life is transformed into death. For this love is love for the sake of God. The beloved who is loved for God's sake is always loved. He is a sovereign of affection enthroned in the heart. This kind of love and affection is a trust from God, Exalted is He, to His servants. He loves His servant and causes him to love; He makes His servant feel affection. While He Himself loves His servant, however, He hides and conceals His love for that servant from his other servants, and does not always make those other servants love the servant He loves. He may sometimes make His beloved loved and respected. But He may sometimes have His servants beaten. When the servant who is being beaten exclaims "Allah! Allah!," He says: "My servant is remembering Me and seeking refuge with Me."

Among His special servants, indeed, did He not have Zakariah, on him be peace, cut up with a saw? Did He not have John, on him be peace, cut to bits? Did He not have Noah, peace be upon him, scourged? Did He not have Abraham, on him be peace, cast into the fire? Did He not have Joseph, on him be peace, thrown into the well, and have him sold as a slave in the market? Did He not make them intend to crucify Jesus, on him be peace? Did He not subject Mary, on her be peace, to slander and calumny? Did He not have Moses, on him be peace, separated from his mother and thrown into the river Nile? Did He not have them smash the tooth of the blessed Prophet Muhammad? Did He not make a thirsting martyr of Imam Hussein, along with his seventy-two friends? Did He not make martyrs of Abu Bakr al-Siddiq by poison, 'Umar al-Faruq and 'Uthman by the dagger, and 'Ali the Impetuous Lion by a poisoned sword, after a hundred thousand afflictions? Did He not take unto Himself and grant union to Imam Hasan through poison, and many other lovers and friends by the chain, cutting off the pure and innocent heads of some, putting some to fire and some to drowning? Indeed, it is sometimes thus that affection appears and manifests itself.

Show Beauty's candle, let the moths burn therein,
Happy the lover's fate, for sure, in such a flame to burn.
The mosque and school to pious hypocrites we leave,
For worshipping the Truth, ruins are all we need.
The sweetheart, velvet-eyed gazelle, has raided my self-esteem;
Make tight the chain of love, let not the crazy flee.
The Wine I'll not forswear, from a rival's hand let me not sup;
Offer me with Thy mighty hand cup upon overflowing cup.
Through all the torture and the pain, Shemsi forsakes Thee not;
That he should tire of loving Thee—such thoughts must be forgot.

Affection toward God, Exalted is He, is possible for the servant through obedience to the object of his love, through wanting nothing more than to be His slave, and by lovingly carrying out His commands and performing the duties of His service. In other words, it is possible by letting oneself fall like a drop into the ocean. It means knowing that you are from God, recognizing that you are with God, that you will be with Him eternally, never forgetting that you are His servant, grateful in word and deed for all the material and spiritual blessings that He has graciously conferred upon you, and aware of your impotence and nothingness.

What is absolutely certain is the truth that spiritual love is incomparably higher in degree than material love. Nevertheless there is a way from material love to spiritual love, from material affection to spiritual affection. Those unable to find this radiant way are left behind in mere matter; they cannot take the road and cannot reach the desired goal. We have tried to take the opportunity of explaining this above. When the qualities and attributes that cause and occasion material affection cease to exist, the affection itself disappears. But spiritual affection is everlasting and enduring.

Look carefully at human history and take a lesson from it. You will see how in most cases material affection has passed away, sometimes forgotten and gathering dust in the faded pages of history books or else, at best, forming the subject matter of novels and stories. On the other hand, how many lovers and friends of Moses, Jesus, and the beloved Prophet Muhammad, peace be upon them, ready and willing to sacrifice their all for them, are still found in the world today and will be found there till the end of time. In our own day, which many call the age of materialism, there are millions whose love of God, Exalted is He, His Messengers, and God's noble loved ones makes them weep night and day with tears of reverent affection. Yet could you find anyone today weeping for Anthony and Cleopatra?

At all events, love and affection, whether material or spiritual, are sacred. We have tried to explain above that spiritual affection is greatly superior to the material kind. For there is an important difference between them. Material affection can often have an ulterior motive.

But spiritual affection is for God's sake, which is why this kind of affection is called love for God's sake. Those whose affection is for God, Exalted is He, must be ready and prepared for every kind of misfortune. In reality, what appears as a misfortune is a very great blessing. The friends of God, Exalted is He, will grieve and lament at those times when no misfortune has befallen them. Misfortune for them is pure joy. It should not be forgotten that the severest afflictions have been reserved for the Prophets, the saints who are the heirs of those Prophets, and those of similar rank in the presence of God. If someone claims to love God, Exalted is He, yet in the face of any misfortune complains of his Lord to other servants and bemoans that misfortune, he lies in making such a claim. Have you not read, have you not heard? The Prophet Job, on him be peace, for all the misfortunes that befell him, his property, and his children, made no complaint and never bemoaned his lot. As a reward for this, God, the Lord of Majesty and Perfection, graciously conferred upon him the rank of Penitent Servant. Besides enduring so many misfortunes for so long, he would seek refuge from God's Majesty with His Beauty. That is, he would shelter from God with God, drawing the Divine Mercy upon himself with the prayer:

"O Lord! A misfortune has befallen me. You are the Most Merciful of the merciful."

One who is sincere in his love for his beloved will be obedient to his loved one. The mark of the sincerely affectionate is not to offend his loved one. The sign of affection is not to complain of the loved one to anybody, to put up with the loved one's whims, and lovingly to carry out the request of the beloved.

This in indeed what the Prophet Job, on him be peace, did. He complained of his Lord to no one. Seeking refuge with his Lord's Beauty from His Majesty, he sheltered from his Lord *with* his Lord. What other door is there to shelter in? To shelter with God from God is not to complain of God, Exalted is He. It is rather to demonstrate and prove to men the true place of refuge. The sincerely affectionate one who claims to love God will never disobey Him and will recoil from offending Him. The lover lovingly obeys his loved one. The true sign of the sincerely affectionate is his following his beloved, obeying his loved one, and carefully avoiding things unwanted and disliked by his loved one. Those who fulfill these conditions have displayed, proclaimed, and proved their affection. This is genuine affection. Anyone who cannot tolerate his loved one's whims, cannot bear the loved one's cruelties, and shows laziness and slackness in the service of the beloved, can definitely and absolutely never be a sincerely affectionate lover.

The venerable Shibli, may his soul be sanctified, was once overtaken by a mystical state and was locked up in a lunatic asylum. Imagining that they loved him, many people went to the asylum to visit him.

"Who are you?" asked Sheikh Shibli.

"We are some of those who love you," they replied.

Shibli began gathering stones from the ground and throwing them at his visitors, whereupon they started to scatter, saying "Alas! The venerable Sheikh has really gone mad."

But he called out to them: "Did I hear you saying that you loved me? You could not even bear my throwing a stone at you, and you began to run away. What became of that sincere love that you had for me? If you had really loved me, you would have put up with this little quirk of mine and would have endured patiently any troubles I might cause you."

So saying, he has taught us a great lesson in affection and enlightened us all on the subject of true affection. Those expert in affection drink the wine of love from the goblet of affection; for them this world, which is really very wide, becomes a narrow place. They love God, Exalted is He, with complete and perfect affection, they really dread and recoil from His majesty and grandeur, they are dazed and amazed by His creative power. They consider His orders a great favor to themselves and a crown of success on their heads. Those who drink the wine of love from His mighty hand and from the cup of affection make merry with Him in the sea of intimate friendship. Through their prayers and supplications, they enjoy His company. This is such contentment, pleasure, and delight that for them night and day, black and white, the world and all therein, rank and title, status and dignity, cease to exist and they are annihilated in God. As for those who are annihilated in God, it is an absolute certainty that they will exist forever.

3

LOVE OF GOD

O my Generous Master!

You created this servant of Yours and brought him into being from a drop of water. I do not even have the right to say I love You, and yet I do love You. I always remember You. I know that even my being able to remember You is also due to Your guidance. My mentioning Your Name of Majesty left me drunk, bewildered, and amazed. Is it possible to imagine anyone in this world loving the Divinity and not becoming intoxicated with such affection? So great a blessing is affection that even if its possessor should stray into the wilderness, the fire of his love would not allow him to feel the heat of the desert. Should the lover fall into the fire, the heat of his love would extinguish that fire. The fire of love would cause the poles and glaciers to melt. If mountains and boulders were piled upon the back of the lover, the fire of his love would prevent his feeling the weight of the load.

Affection makes a person forget about hunger and thirst, and keeps him on the road of love. All creatures have taken their allotted share of affection. Even animals, when they are in love, will go for days without eating and drinking. That poor beast the camel, when love goes to his head, will eat no food for forty days. While in this state, he can be made to carry many times his normal load. His inclination and desire for his darling render him immune to whatever kind of pain and torment he may suffer, so that he ignores it and does not even feel it.

Let us think and speak fairly:

If the affection felt by the lovelorn camel—just an animal, after all—is such that he will give up eating and drinking because of it and endure such agony and suffering, what kind of evidence, what sort of proof can those who claim to have affection for God, Exalted is He, show to prove this affection of theirs? Have they been able to give up whatever has been forbidden by God, Exalted is He, Whom they say they love? Lovers cannot doze off in the presence of their beloved. How many nights have they spent without sleep for the sake of God? How many days have they been able to go without food and drink for the sake of their affection for God, Exalted is He? For how many days have they been able to endure hardship, difficulty, and trouble for the sake of that True Beloved?

My dear friend:

Are you ready to sacrifice yourself, your property, your rank and station, even your children, for the sake of your beloved? If you have not been, and will not be, able to do as much, then your pretension and your claim to affection stem from nothing but falsehood and hypocrisy. One who has affection for Almighty God must sacrifice himself for the sake of his beloved. Such is the symbol of affection. Be it Hell itself, the truly affectionate is capable of preferring above Paradise the place to which his beloved invites him. Should the loved one summon him to death, he can regard that death as better than life itself.

Ibrahim Hawwas was asked about the nature and meaning of love and affection for God, Exalted is He. This is what he said:

"It is to expel and erase from the heart everything unwanted and unloved by God, the Lord of Majesty and Perfection, to burn to ashes all bad qualities, attributes and desires for the sake of the command and will of the True Beloved, to cleanse the self in the ocean of spiritual knowledge, and to enlighten it with the radiance of affection."

We have said that the feeling called affection is the condition resulting from the heart's inclination toward all that we find pleasing and delightful to our nature. When this condition settles in the heart and grows intense, it is known as the Sovereign Power of Love. The lover will sacrifice for the beloved reason, logic, and interest, will obey the beloved in perfect bondage, will be ready to sacrifice everything he has for the loved one's sake. The rule and principle "Whatever the lover has is ransom for the beloved" can be brought to its perfect fulfillment through Love.

One who cannot lay down his life for his darling has no business pretending to the title of lover. In the illustrious Sura *Yusuf* of the Noble Koran, which He calls the Best of Stories, God, Exalted and Sanctified is He, relates the tale of the fabulously beautiful wife of Potiphar of Egypt, and how—because of the love she bore for Joseph, on him be peace—she "smashed the bottle of shame and modesty" and sacrificed her wealth, her property, her status, her honor and good name, all her valuables amounting to seventy camel-loads of gold, silver, diamonds and pearls, rubies and emeralds, her palaces and her power. History records how she used to shower priceless jewels upon anyone who brought her tidings of Joseph, on him be peace, or said to her: "I saw Joseph!" So great was her love for Joseph, on him be peace, that she gave and gave until she had nothing left. She would call Joseph's name. She would see Joseph, on him be peace, amid the stars in the sky, and imagined his name was inscribed on the sun and the moon.

This is how it really is. The lover sees everyone as his beloved; wherever he looks he beholds the name and form of his loved one, and he does not hesitate to sacrifice his every possession in this cause.

Zulaykha was really enamored of God, Exalted is He. The Divine Truth had become manifest to her through Joseph, on him be peace. Fundamentally, all loves relate and refer to the True Beloved. However, the manifestations appear variously. The lover witnesses this manifestation in his beloved. Thus he who is wise does not stop at metaphorical love, but sooner or later atttains to True Love. The lover sees in his loved one the True Beloved. The one he loves is a veil on the True Beloved, so that once he can rend this veil the True Beloved becomes apparent to him. As they say:

The sign of love once gained,
The Beloved must be attained.

Zulaykha therefore sacrificed her all for the sake of Joseph, on him be peace, and, her youth and beauty at last restored by Divine Decree, she came to be united with the Joseph by whom she had been faithfully honored as soon as he saw her face. And yet, once married to Joseph, on him be peace, she took to escaping from him. She would withdraw to desolate and lonely places, there to worship her beloved God in solitude. When Joseph, on him be peace, called her to bed, she would promise to come the next day, if it was night, or the next night, if it was day. Joseph, on him be peace, would say to her: "Why do you run away from me? You are now my lawful wife. Once upon a time I used to run from you when you called me to your bed, for then you were unlawful to me. I excused myself from accepting your invitations for fear of disobedience to my Lord. But now at last you are my lawful wife. Does one flee from one's lawful spouse?"

To this Zulaykha would reply: "O Joseph the Truthful! I used to love you before I came to know God, Exalted is He. But now it is no longer you I love. It seems you were the veil upon the One I really loved. Now I have rent that veil and discovered my Lord. Since I found God,

Exalted is He, and got to know Him, His love has conquered my heart. It has expelled from my heart all other loves. His love wants no love in its place, and nought but His love intoxicates me."

I wonder if I make my meaning plain?

They asked Majnun his name. "Layla," said he without a moment's thought.

> They asked Majnun where was Layla's abode;
> Tearing his breast, his ruined heart he showed.

When Layla died, they said to Majnun: "Layla is dead." But Majnun retorted: "No! Layla is not dead. She is in my heart. See, I am Layla!"

One day, Majnun came to Layla's village; on reaching the front of her house, he began gazing at the heavens. "Don't look at the sky," they said to him. "Watch the walls of Layla's house. Maybe Layla's form will be reflected there and you will have seen your Layla." But he replied:

> They asked Majnun: Was Layla the same?
> Layla had gone, though they still spoke her name;
> Into my heart a new Layla now came.
> Layla begone, for the Lord I have found.
>
> Who now sees the Lord, looks at Layla no longer,
> Who now sees the great, looks at rabble no longer,
> Who now sees the moon, at the star looks no longer.
> Layla begone, for the Lord I have found.
>
> Majnun with longing to the Kaaba came;
> Once in the circle, moaning shook his frame.
> Majnun found God while uttering Layla's name.
> Layla begone, for the Lord I have found.

Majnun was served by slaves and maids, the best;
On Majnun's head the birds now make themselves a nest,
Mountains and plains have now become our place of rest.
Layla begone, for the Lord I have found.

Over the mountain, crazy, I go reeling;
With God alone I'll from now on be dealing.
Come, Layla, for I weary of this passionate feeling.
Layla begone, for the Lord I have found.

Great birds on my head their nests did array.
I dreamed of the Lord while sleeping I lay.
Away with you, Layla, don't stand in my way,
Layla begone, for the Lord I have found.

O Yunus, come, these mysteries do not forsake,
God's grace once seen, no other can you take;
Do not desert the place of Truth, for goodness' sake.
Layla begone, for the Lord I have found.

My Lord, lead us all from imitation to verification, from metaphorical love to Real Love; bring us into the company and fellowship of the true lovers; let us share the affection of those whose love is such that for its sake they sacrifice body and soul.

Yes! By way of Layla the Lord is reached. From the idol we turn to the Everlasting. From the ascription of partners to God we come to recognize His Oneness. From metaphorical love we move on to Real Love. To the human being, love is absolutely necessary. This love, be it metaphorical or Real, is a feeling and attribute proper to mankind. One devoid of love is indistinguishable from the ass.

In Istanbul, construction of the noble Beyazid mosque had been completed and a ceremony was to be held to mark its opening for public worship. Out of all the contemporary scholars, men distinguished in the field of practical and spiritual science, Sultan Beyazid Khan II had vouchsafed to designate one of the Halveti Sheikhs, the venerable Jemaleddin Halveti, to conduct the ceremony. The venerable Sheikh mounted the pulpit in order to perform this sacred duty. The military and civilian chiefs, headed by the Sultan and Grand Vizier in person, the foremost scholars of the age, and a vast congregation filled the noble mosque. The venerable Jemaleddin Halveti was about to start his speech, when up stood a member of the congregation, saying:

"O reverend Sheikh! I came here intent on joining this bountiful gathering. But due to the overcrowding you can see, I have lost my donkey. As the whole congregation is here assembled in readiness to listen to your sagacious person, I wonder if I might not enquire of those present whether or not they have seen an ownerless donkey, the characteristics of which I shall describe?"

The venerable Sheikh replied, with a gentle smile:

"My brother for the sake of God! Have patience and you'll find your donkey, God willing."

Then he added, addressing those assembled:

"O congregation! Is there among you anyone who does not know what love is, and who has never loved anything in his whole life?"

Someone stood up amid the congregation and said:

"O Sheikh! I do not know what love is; to this day I have never loved anything and have never been able to love."

When two others had joined the first who did not know what love was, and who said he had never loved anything, the venerable Jemaleddin Halveti addressed the person who had lost his donkey:

"You said you had lost a donkey of yours. Look, I have found you no fewer than three. The only difference is that the one you lost was a quadruped, whereas these are two-legged."

He then proceeded with his sermon.

We absolve and exonerate the faithful, and we assert and confirm the existence of God's love and affection, and the affection of God's Messenger, in the hearts of all the believers, their hearts being illuminated by the light of faith. However, this ought not to be forgotten: As a warning to those who suppose that love is nothing more than the product of lust and animal instincts, we consider it worthwhile to explain that on such an interpretation the donkey would be the very highest creature. Love and lust should never be confused with one another.

We have said that intense affection is called Love. Inasmuch as that affection is fondness, liking, and self-extinction in the dear one, its extreme form, Love, is in one respect a subdivision of madness. One afflicted with the sickness of Love is called a Lover.

There are two categories of Lovers: (1) the lover suffering from metaphorical love and (2) the lover smitten with Real Love.

One afflicted with Real Love is called a Lover in God. These are the lovers of Allah, Glorified and Exalted is He. This group consists of the angels, the Messengers of Almighty God, and the saints who are their heirs. The righteous of the community are also candidates for this group.

Metaphorical love is where a man has an extreme affection for a woman and loses himself in his beloved. However, metaphorical love leads to Real Love. While calling "Layla, Layla!" Majnun was united with his Lord. As we have tried to explain just above, we should pity anyone stuck with Layla and not finding his Lord. For it means that his Layla veils his Lord and in a sense becomes his misfortune.

The real name of the legendary Majnun was Qays. He was given the name—or rather, the nickname—Majnun because of his love and affection for Layla. Such was his love for Layla that on arriving in his beloved's village he would kiss the eyes and feet of the village dogs, saying to those who tried to deter him from this behavior:

"Leave me alone! These eyes have seen Layla. These feet have trodden where Layla walked. Eyes that have seen her and feet that have trodden in her footsteps are sacred to me and worthy of being kissed."

To those who said: "Layla is a swarthy, skinny, very ugly girl! Let us find you a prettier one, a gazelle-eyed, willowy Layla," he gave this reply: "If you saw my Layla through my eyes, you would not be making me that kind of proposal."

Majnun means "crazy." Qays's nickname was Majnun, or the madman of his Layla. But it was quite correct, in fact, for a genuine lover to love his beloved in this way. For the passion of love manifests itself in accordance with each person's makeup and constitution. In those who are human in form, but merely animal in character, love assumes the appearance of lust. Those impassioned with such bestial instincts will abandon the loved one as soon as they have achieved their desire; for the desired object has been attained, and lustful passions stilled. This is not love, but lust, greed, and appetite. The likes of these can often kill without a qualm the very ones whose lovers they were supposed to be. The many homicide cases that appear in the headlines as crimes of passion bear witness to the common occurrence in all parts of the world of addicts to lust masquerading as love.

Love within the institution of the family, between husband and wife, is not the product and result of sensual desires. It is something divine and holy, far transcending animal instincts. Consequently, we must never confuse the sacred love within the family institution with the false and ephemeral liaisons we have described above as prompted by the urging of animal instincts.

In animal and sensual liaisons appearing in the guise of love, jealousy sometimes reaches such a pitch that the lover may quite easily kill the one he loves. Indeed, such cases come to our notice every day.

This should come as no surprise. For such loves can also occur among animals themselves. For instance, the dog of the house will be jealous of another dog liked by his owner, and will try to bite it and drive it away from his master if he can. Failing this, it is even possible—and known to happen—that he will dare to bite his own master. This behavior on the dog's part is the result of jealousy appearing in the guise of love.

At the same time, there are also genuine lovers among the animals. Experiments have proved that certain predators are loving by nature.

There is a kind of jealousy in Real Love. However, this jealousy must be distinguished from ordinary jealousy. For while ordinary jealousy is the attribute of one who is imperfect, jealousy with a capital *J* is a quality manifest in one who is complete.

Our master, the most noble Messenger, God bless him and give him peace, once said to 'Umar al-Faruq, may God be pleased with him: "O 'Umar! You are Jealous. I am more Jealous than you. God in His Majesty is more Jealous than I."

Therefore Jealousy is an acceptable and praiseworthy attribute. This attribute in God, Exalted and Sanctified is He, is the quality of Perfection, and He trained His beloved Prophet to be characterized by this quality.

God, Glorified and Exalted is He, is endowed with the qualities of perfection and devoid of all attributes of deficiency. For His servants, to be characterized by some of the attributes peculiar to God, Exalted is He, is the greatest blessing and good fortune.

O seeker after the Truth!

God the Truth, the All-Munificent, is Jealous. He does not want His beloved servants to love anything but His Divine Essence. For the true and real Beloved is none but He. To be loved is the right of His Unitary Essence. Should lovers of His Unitary Essence give their hearts to anything but Him, misfortune would surely befall them. It is therefore necessary for those who love God, Exalted is He, to love nothing other than God, Exalted is He. At least, they must not regard what they love as other than God, since what makes them see the Truth in what they love is essentially nought but He. All goodness, all special qualities, everything we love is His work.

One who loves the effect must surely love the cause as well. Therefore the wise can never separate the effect and the true cause from each other. As the Word of God became manifest to Moses, on him be peace, from Mount Sinai, so for the lover the object of his love is like Mount Sinai. The goodness and special qualities he sees there are the manifestation of the True Friend and Beloved in the presence and being of his loved one.

Therefore, do not stick at the effect; come to the cause! Do not stay with the names; come to what is named! Do not stop at the word; come to the meaning!

One day, our master the glorious Prophet, to him and his family the most excellent salutations, sat his grandsons Hasan and Hussein upon his blessed knees, tenderly caressing and loving them. It so happened that his pure and noble daughter, Fatima the Radiant, may God be pleased with her, had sewn up the shirt collars of those two blessed children too tight, having mistaken them for the legs of her trousers. Seeing them both suffering discomfort from this, the chief of the Prophets unbuttoned the collars of those two princes. At that moment he shuddered as he realized that his affection for his dear grandsons had reached the degree of his love for God, Exalted is He, so that he had actually incurred God's Jealousy.

Just then Gabriel, on him be peace, descended with three shawls in his hand, one yellow, one red, and one black, conveyed to the Beloved of the Almighty the greetings of God, Exalted and Sanctified is He, and divulged the divine command, or rather, the arcane mysteries:

"O Messenger of the Messengers! God, Magnified and Glorified is He, sends His salutations to the bearer of His Mission, and says: 'How can it be that he who loves Me and whom I love, My dearly loved friend, My beloved, should kiss his grandchildren, his offspring, with love and affection equal in degree to his love for Me? This yellow shawl I have sent for Hasan, the red one for Hussein, and the black for the honored Messenger. Let each put on his shawl. Black is the mark of mourning and funerals. Hasan will be martyred by poison, Hussein by the dagger. Since he kissed Hasan on the mouth and Hussein on the neck, their fates have been determined thus." He then withdrew to his station.

In reality, matters turned out just so. Imam Hasan, may God be pleased with him, was martyred by poison at his wife's hand, while Imam Hussein met his martyrdom in the tragedy of Karbala', his head cut off with a dagger.

Ibrahim Adham, sanctified be his most noble spirit, said:

"I chanced to meet a certain individual in the mountains of Lebanon. During forty days we spent together, this individual ate not a morsel of food, nor drank a drop of water. I was quite at a loss to understand this strange condition of his. Eventually, a rogue camel appeared, trampled his head, and crushed him to death. As a result of the camel's knocking and kicking, his eyes popped out of their sockets. While I was pondering and reflecting in bewilderment over this sad fate of his, I received this information through divine inspiration:

"'If one who is My lover looks at any but Me, see how I crush his head and take out his eyes.'

"I then understood that his very holy person had looked upon his beloved as other than God."

Ibrahim Adham, sanctified be his most noble spirit, chose the throne of the heart in preference to the throne of empire, so he went to settle in Mecca the Ennobled. Many a long year had gone by since he had abdicated from the throne in favor of his son and left his country behind, and during that time his son had grown into a very handsome and comely youth. Then one day he learned that his son, as his country's sovereign, had come to Mecca the Ennobled with zealous intent to perform the religious duty of Pilgrimage. The venerable Ibrahim Adham made his way to the revered Kaaba in order to catch one more glimpse of his son, albeit from afar, with his earthly eyes. Scanning the pilgrims as they made their circumambulation, he straightaway spotted his son in the midst of the throng and his blood raced with excitement. In one instant, he realized that his love and affection for his son had risen to the rank of the love he bore for God, Exalted is He, and bursting into tears right then and there he uttered this supplication:

"O Lord! I am incapable of uniting in the same heart both the love and affection I hold for Your Divine Essence and that I feel for my son, whose face I have not even seen all these years."

Before the words were out of his mouth, the Lord of the Universe, Who is the True Beloved, vouchsafed an answer to this prayer: The young sovereign fell right there as he made his circumambulation, and yielded up his spirit to God.

O sincere lover!

You must know that if you can see God in your beloved, you will be saved from the sin of associating partners with Him. But if you divide love in two—with God is our refuge!—you fall into this sin of association. Love of God admits of no partnership; love of Creator and love of creature cannot be united in the same heart. If you attach your property and your children to yourself, some calamity will attach them to God. If you know God to be the cause, glad be the tidings—how happy for you!

Everything is He. Love is He. The lover is He. The beloved is He. The dear one is He. The sought-for is He. The intended is He. Apart from Him there is nothing. The seer is He, the seen is He, your essence is He, your speech is He, all is He, all is from Him.

Many are the lovers of God who have surrendered to Him in the way of love, have abandoned themselves and attained the Beloved, have rejoiced with the Beloved. Because of neglectfulness toward his Beloved, was not Abraham, on him be peace, commanded to slaughter his own son?

Yes, those who are lovers of God, Exalted is He, must be ready and prepared for trials. This love is a trial such that it is pleasure and delight within tribulation. Because he was a lover of God, Abraham, on him be peace, was cast into the fire, yet for him Nimrod's fiery furnace suddenly turned into light. Because of it, those who fall into the fire become the friends and intimates of God.

If you are the Loved One's lover,
Beware of falling for any other.
Plunge, like Abraham, into the flame;
In this rose garden it causes no pain.

So leave the rest and cleave to love! Turn your heart from all else; feel love in your whole personality! Take love as your guide and leader to the land of being, so that you may reach the True Beloved, enter the Paradise of essence, behold the beauty of the Friend, gather the roses of the garden of Union. In the way of love, the lover sacrifices himself but finds the dear one. All the saints who have come and gone and drunk of the wine of love, all have sacrificed themselves thus in the way of love. Have you not heard what happened to Mansur al-Hallaj? Have you never read how, in the way of love, his body was burned and his ashes strewn on the Tigris? Did no one ever tell you how each atom of his body came to touch a lover, burning and inflaming them with that same fire of love?

Mansur al-Hallaj was imprisoned by people who could not understand the secret of the words ANA-L-HAQQ that appeared on his tongue. The venerable Shibli went to visit him and asked him the hidden meaning of his strange behavior:

"O Mansur! What is Love?"

Mansur al-Hallaj said with a smile:

"I shall be able to give an answer to that question tomorrow."

The following day they brought al-Hallaj to the gallows. He called out to Sheikh Shibli, who was among the crowd that had come to watch:

"O Shibli! Love begins with burning, and ends in dying thus."

Mansur al-Hallaj was such a lover of Truth that his eyes never saw anything other than God, Exalted is He. This condition caused him even to forget himself. It was for this reason that he said ANA-L-HAQQ. Otherwise, he could never have said such a thing of his own will and desire. When he said ANA-L-HAQQ, he had become intoxicated by the Truth, *haqq*. In reality, these words that appeared on his tongue were the speech of God, *haqq*.

Just as the words INNI ANA-LLAH, "Indeed I am God," which came to Moses, on him be peace, from the fire on Mount Sinai, did not really issue from that blessed burning bush, for the same reason the words of Mansur al-Hallaj, "I am *haqq*," were really the speech of God. The word *haqq* was used here as an adjective, the opposite of which would be *batil*, false.

They asked Junayd al-Baghdadi, sanctified be his spirit:

"What did Mansur al-Hallaj mean by saying ANA-L-HAQQ, 'I am the True'?"

The venerable Junayd replied:

"What else could he have said? Could he have said: *Ana-l-batil*, 'I am the false'?"

The word *haqq* did not only mean God. For example, in the expressions: "Paradise is *haqq*, Hell is *haqq*, the Questioning is *haqq*, the Reckoning and the Balance are *haqq*," there is no doubt that the word *haqq* does not signify God. Although everybody knows this to be so, they interpreted al-Hallaj's words "I am *haqq*" in the sense of God, and on that account they put him to death. According to our understanding, he suffered the gibbet in the way of Truth for the sake of the Truth, in the way of love for the sake of love, and became the chief of those who are lovers of God, Exalted is He:

> The words of those intoxicated come not from themselves, my friend,
> But then how many say ANA-L-HAQQ, without their being Mansur!

To those who asked Mansur al-Hallaj: "Who are you?" he would reply: "I am *haqq*." To those who asked: "What is your name?" he would reply: "My name is *haqq*."

In this way and with this claim, he gave his life in love's cause and set the pattern for those who are Lovers in God. Therefore, those who are Lovers in God have made it the litany of their tongues and the latch of their hearts.

Genuine love, genuine fondness, becomes apparent through three conditions found in the genuine lover:

1. To the lover, every word, every wish, every command of the one whose lover he is seems like a crown, a remedy for his aching heart; he considers it the greatest favor and good fortune and accomplishes it at once, always giving it priority over the words and desires of others.

2. He always prefers to be at the side of his beloved, inseparably, rather than to be with others.

3. That his beloved should be pleased and content with him matters more to him than the pleasure of others.

If you are really a lover of Truth, therefore, you must always and everywhere prefer God's word to the words of men. If you love God, be with Him and find Him in yourself however you are and whatever you are doing. Remove from your heart whatever is other than Him, and place in your heart no affection for any but Him. Be ever in search of His pleasure and desirous of His beauty.

And don't forget this!

Love is rending the veils. Love is unraveling the mysteries and seeing the beauty of the Beloved here and now. Those too blind to see the beauty of the Beloved here and now will be blind tomorrow in the Hereafter, and will be unable to behold the beauty of the Beloved.

> Hear what Niyazi has to say:
> Nothing hides the face of God away;
> Apart from God nothing is manifest,
> Though the eyeless suppose him invisible.

Love makes us penetrate the mountains. Love makes us reach the goal. Love causes ecstasy. Ecstasy, being the state in which love and longing overwhelm the soul, gives the taste to the dhikr of the worshipper. Such a state is this, that if at that moment one of the worshipper's limbs were to be cut off or broken, he would not even feel the pain amid the joy and delight occasioned by his vision of the everlasting Beauty, as he performs his dhikr with ecstasy of love and longing. Since, when they come to death, lovers find themselves in union with the Divine Beauty, the lover does not feel the pain of the spirit's parting from the body, so deep is his delight at being with his Beloved.

One of the friends of God once saw a pale young man weeping and moaning by the revered Kaaba. He approached him and asked him what was the matter with him.

"I am in love!" said the young man.

The friend of God took pity on the young man's condition, saying:

"Tell me who she is; let me just fetch the girl you love, whoever she may be."

But the young man, moaning amid his tears, recited this couplet:

> Attachment to any but God would only be an excess;
> I love the Beauty Everlasting, Allah be my witness.

As soon as that respected person, realizing that the young man was a lover of God, said: "I too am a lover of that Dear One," the youth gave a cry of "Allah!" and there and then attained his goal. He met with his Lord, came together with the object of his desire.

That friend of God said: "I immediately covered him over and went out of the Sacred Mosque to look for a few people to carry away that blessed corpse. But when I came back, nowhere could I find the body of that happy and fortunate young man. As I looked about me, saying in my surprise and amazement 'Glory to God! I wonder what has happened,' a voice called from the unseen:

"'O Friend! Why are you surprised and amazed at being unable to find that lover? Such was the nature of that young man that Satan sought him for years with a view to deceiving him, but could not find him in this world. Malik, the guardian of Hell, looked for him and he could not find him either. Ridwan, the guardian of Paradise, looked for him and he could not find him either.'

"'O Lord. Please be so kind as to tell this impotent slave of Yours: In that case, where is the young man?'

"'Because his love and affection for Us grew with every breath he took throughout his entire life, because of his sincerity in service and obedience to Us, and because he at once repented and asked forgiveness for any rebellion or forgetfulness, We, the Almighty, the Sole Possessor of Power, have joined him to the band of the truthful ones, who are entertained in the presence of the Omnipotent King, in the council of the Truth; and We have honored him in the country of the lovers.'"

When the wise were asked the mark and sign of lovers, this was their reply:

"Lovers converse with people only as much as they need to. For the most part, they prefer to be alone and by themselves. For they yearn for intimate communion with the Beloved. They are constantly in meditation. They do not enjoy excessive conversation and always prefer not to talk. They do not understand conversation about anything other than God. When they encounter some misfortune, they do not grumble and complain. They know that misfortune comes from the Friend, and see the benefits contained in a thing which has the appearance of a misfortune. Divine Love has possessed them, and they have plunged lovingly into the fire of love. Going barefoot, bareheaded, and poorly clad does not worry them at all. Their eyes are sore from weeping, their breasts are seared by the fire of love. They hear no words but the words of God. They never desist from the remembrance of God. Apart from God they are afraid of nothing. Everywhere they behold God's Beauty. On familiar terms with God, Glorified and Exalted is He, they commune with Him alone. They do not haggle and quarrel with worldly people over worldly things; they share their love and affection with no one. Their aim is God alone and their desire is God's good pleasure."

Jesus, on him be peace, one day saw a young man watering the garden and he greeted him with peace. The young man recognized Jesus, on him be peace, and said:

"O Messenger of God! Pray for me to the Almighty that He may grant as my portion one atom of His love."

Jesus replied: "Know for sure that you could not bear as much as the one atom of God's love you so desire."

But the young man insisted: "In that case, let Him grant me just half an atom of His love."

Jesus, the Spirit of God, raised his hands once in supplication to the Divine Unity: "O Lord! Grant and bestow upon this youth just half an atom of Your love." Then he went on his way.

Sometime later, Jesus, on him be peace, passed that way again; he could not see the young man who had begged him for just half an atom of God's love, so he asked where he was. They said:

"O Prophet of God! That young man went away to the mountains and wandered into the deserts. We have no news of how he is and what has become of him."

Jesus, on him be peace, prayed to the Almighty and asked for that young man to be shown to him. By divine inspiration, Jesus, on him be peace, was told the young man's whereabouts and he went straight there. Seeing the youth sitting on a steep rock, immersed in contemplation, he called out to him. Far from responding, the young man did not even turn his head and look. Jesus, on him be peace, called out again, identifying himself this time, but again he got no response. It was then that God, the Lord of Majesty and Perfection, vouchsafed to Jesus, on him be peace, this inspiration:

"How can one with even half an atom of My love in his heart be expected to hear the voices of men? O Jesus! For the sake of My Might and Majesty, do not suppose that he heard your voice and yet gave you no answer. If they were to cut that young man up with a saw, he would feel no pain. If they threw him into the fire, the fire would not burn his body, and he would not even notice the heat of the flames."

O sincere lover!

Following love's guidance, the people of Reality attain Real Love, meet with the Real Lover, and remain with Him forever. Love is the source of all forms of knowledge. Love is the source of all created beings. For love's sake, all these entities, beings, and intelligibles have been created and formed as lovers. If you move on from the station, you will reach the Lord of the station.

The Real Beloved is the very self of love and of the lover, There is nothing prior to love. Love is the first of the first. Love is the last of the last. The ultimate is the perfect self of love outer and inner, its essence. After everything has come to nought and perished, love still endures and will endure forever. It is eternal, and will be so for all eternity. Love is without end.

Love is an ocean. Such an ocean it is, that this sea has no bottom, no shore, no beginning, no end, and no limits.

Those blessed with the ability to understand this mystery, those able to attain the grace and good fortune to be capable of possessing this divine favor, only they can have knowledge of this secret. Those who achieve the happiness of being able to drink of this divine wine of love will never quench their thirst by drinking it. The more they drink, the more parched they become, and their dryness will not go away. With love, there is no being replete, no being sated. With love, there is no having plenty, no having had one's fill.

The eternally eternal endures as love and lover-beloved. For the seer can no more satiate himself with seeing than the drinker can satiate himself with drinking.

O Lord!

Letting Your guidance escort us, offer us with Your mighty hand the drinking-glass of love, so that our hearts may never for even one moment be parted from Your love. May they never be separated from Your affection. If those who love You are separated for a split second from Your affection, it is pointless for them to go on living. For Your lovers, You alone are life eternal, life everlasting, life perpetual. It is Your blessed and cherished love. In reality, nothing exists apart from You and what You love. If, as the result of our heedlessness and ignorance, we should love in some other aspect, take that aspect from our hearts and from our eyes, and tell us Whose lover we really ought to be. Show us how and for Whom love should be, and make us taste that flavor. All affection is for You alone; all loves are for Your sake. Allot and bestow the rending and discarding of the veils of the loves that veil You and Your Perfect Beauty, the tasting of the taste of genuine love, and the adding of love to our love, so that we may know Who the True Beloved is, that we may be with Your love in both worlds, and that we may never be parted from it. Only You, my God, shall teach us and show us this secret!

Through divine love, Hell becomes Paradise for the lover. Love turns the fire into light. When the lover enters Paradise, he burns with Your love till Paradise is like Hell for him. Those who burn with divine love feel neither the heat of Hell nor the countless blessings of Paradise, nor yet the pains and pleasures of this world and the Next. They taste only love, see only love, know only love. They actually *are* love. Just as iron heats to a bright red fiery glow when it falls into the fire, so does one who falls into love turn into love. That is why all the friends of God, the saints, and even the Prophets have acknowledged love as their spiritual guide, have adopted love as their religious leader.

O seeker after love!

We have said that unless there is metaphorical love, Real Love will not be found. Real Love is reached by way of metaphorical love. Many saints, indeed, have arrived at Real Love by passing through metaphorical love. And then lovers who die of metaphorical love, since they cross over to the Other World in a state of love, are even classed as martyrs by virtue of their mode of death and attain the rank of martyrdom.

As for the Messengers and those friends of God who are His intimates, since they are always in direct communion there is for them no further need of metaphorical love.

Yes, metaphorical love is the path that leads to Real Love. All that is required of the lover is that he rend the veil of metaphorical love and attain to Real Love. Metaphorical love is a veil of light. It resembles patience and abstinence. That is why the venerable Shems flung noble Mevlana's books into the pond. Our venerable Master, Jelaluddin Rumi, had an excessive fondness and affection for his books, which were an obstacle and a veil between him and Real Love. In a sense, his books were a veil of light separating him from his Lord and His love.

As well as a veil of light, there can also exist between lover and beloved a veil of darkness. The veil of darkness is formed of the sins we commit; it is possible to rend and remove this veil by means of repentance.

As for the veil of light, this can be torn asunder by witnessing the power of God in all things. This is a Divine Grace, for unless God, Exalted and Sanctified is He, is the lover of His servant, the servant cannot be the lover of the Truth. As one who is in metaphorical love comes to realize wherefore and why he is a lover, and Whose lover he is, he turns from metaphorical love to Real Love.

We can define metaphorical love by means of a parable:

Imagine a great mountain adorned with trees and flowers. The interior of this mountain is full of gold and precious stones. Someone seeing only the surface of the mountain, its trees and flowers, or—to put it more clearly—its external appearance, will be at first entranced and then enamored. Being unable to perceive the gold and precious stones within the mountain, he cannot discern its interior and remains on the outside. Just so with metaphorical love. Only when one begins to perceive the beauty within the womb of the mountain does he pass on from metaphorical love to Real Love.

Rend the veil of metaphor, therefore, so that you may come to awareness of realities. If you stop short at the beauty of the outer, what appeals to eye and heart will wither and fade and, sooner or later, vanish away. Real Love, on the other hand, is ever young and vital. It neither decays nor perishes. The point is, then, that you should not stick merely to the outside. Outer and inner are both beautiful. You should not think of them as separate, but see them as one. If you see double, you go cross-eyed, and one who aspires to be a lover must not be cross-eyed.

We have already made some mention of the story of Joseph, on him be peace. Returning to this subject, let us consider how God, Mighty and Glorious is He, Who deigns to guide and inform us by telling us the most beautiful and instructive stories, relates the events in the noble Sura *Yusuf* of the Koran, the Decisive Proof:

Zulaykha, the wife of Potiphar, the governor of Egypt, fell in love with Joseph, on him be peace, whom he had bought as a slave in the market. But this love did not remain a secret—all of Egyptian society heard about it and it became the talk of the town. Insidious rumor and ugly gossip began to go the rounds.

So great was Zulaykha's love for Joseph, on him be peace, that although the things being said about her were apparently detrimental, far from hurting her feelings they actually made her happy. For she took pride in that love of hers. Those who are genuinely in love derive a special pleasure from having their love proclaimed. Under any circumstances whatever, they are simply delighted at having their love spoken about and having their names linked. At bottom, the full flavor of love is lost unless the lover "smashes the bottle of shame and modesty."

As we have more than once used the expression "to smash the bottle of shame and modesty," it seems appropriate to explain this saying a bit more fully. Love is essentially a mystery and should always be kept secret. The revelation of a secret that ought to be hidden is at variance with morality and manners. Because of the violent intensity of his love, however, the lover does not conform to this rule and usually takes it upon himself to display his love. By disclosing his love, which is really a secret to be hidden, he violates the norms of society, makes his secret public, and consequently "smashes the bottle of shame and modesty." Since hiding the secret is a human and moral obligation, it follows that its disclosure—being the opposite—is a sin. This is the construction that should be put upon the expression "smashing the bottle of shame and modesty" as employed by certain Sufis; it should not be taken to imply that they disregard all notions of decency and modesty.

Yes, whatever the lover possesses is ransom for the beloved. Be it wealth, life, honor, dignity, rank, status, position, title, it is the lover's pride and glory to sacrifice all for the sake of love. Zulaykha paid no attention to all the gossip; she took no notice of the rumors against her. And yet there is a limit to human patience. The time had come to demonstrate how false and unfounded this gossip was, to let it be seen with whom she was in love, to silence these wagging tongues by putting them to shame. To this end, she invited the prominent society ladies of Egypt to a banquet at her house. She served them fruit and presented each with a sharp knife to peel the fruit. As soon as the society gossips had picked up their knives to peel their fruit, she summoned Joseph, on him be peace, and showed him to the ladies present.

Suddenly faced with the peerless beauty of Joseph, on him be peace, whom they had not seen or known before, the ladies were confused about what to do; as they could not take their eyes off him, and supposing that they were cutting their fruit, they all without exception cut their own hands. However, such was the awed bewilderment of those ladies when faced with the beauty of Joseph, on him be peace, that as they gazed at him in profound admiration none of them felt the pain in their cut and bleeding hands; unable to contain themselves, they cried out involuntarily:

"This is no human being. An angel no less."

I wonder how those ladies, left speechless and dumbfounded before the beauty of Joseph, on him be peace, would have been if they had seen the Beauty of Joseph's Lord? I leave the answer to this question to your own insight and perceptivity.

Our master, the Almighty's beloved Prophet, to him and his family the most excellent of salutations, was nailing his clogs one day. Seeing the pearl-like beads of sweat dripping from his blessed forehead, the Mother of the Believers, Aisha the Truthful, may God be pleased with her and with her father, recited a poem of which the sense was as follows:

"When the women of Egypt beheld the beauty of Joseph, on him be peace, they cut their own hands in amazement and yet felt no pain. O beloved of God! Were they to see this beauty of yours, they would cut their hearts to pieces and still feel no pain."

At this, the most noble Messenger, God bless him and give him peace, joyfully exclaimed:

"My little fair one! You have made me glad and happy."

All Messengers are beautiful. There is no such thing as an ugly Messenger. Adam, and then Joseph, peace be upon them, were particularly beautiful. But our master, the Almighty's dear friend, was the most beautiful of them all. For he was the Mirror of the Truth. One who looked on him would behold the Truth in that radiance, in that mirror.

> This world is a mirror, all things through the Truth exist.
> In the mirror of Muhammad, God is seen to persist.

O sincere lover!

Through loving Joseph, on him be peace, with the desire and longing to make him the instrument of her lust and animal instincts, Zulaykha became the slave of her self, and—losing her property because of this—she became impoverished in all respects. As for Joseph, on him be peace, through his obedience to God, Exalted is He, and his servitude to his Lord, he became the ruler of Egypt. In other words, those who become the slaves of their own selves—be they rulers like Zulaykha—are at length brought low, while those who master their own selves—be they slaves like Joseph, on him be peace—rise in the end to sovereignty and power. Moreover, they do not stop at sovereignty in this world only, but become sovereigns in both worlds and beloved of the All-Merciful.

With the passage of time, Zulaykha's rosy face had withered and faded, her beauty had vanished, lost were the love-locks that once hanged her lovers, her pearly teeth were gone. Her transient external beauty was no more. But her enduring beauty lay in her utter sincerity. To that beauty there was no end.

Riding through the streets of Egypt one day, Joseph, on him be peace, encountered Zulaykha and recognized her at once. Realizing that the lady, whose slave he had been when she was the world's greatest beauty, had fallen into this state because of her love for him, had "smashed the bottle of shame and modesty" and sacrificed her all for the sake of her beloved, he approached Zulaykha and asked about her condition and health. Zulaykha had passed through metaphorical love to Real Love, had found in Joseph, on him be peace, the opportunity of witnessing the skill and power of the Lord and Creator of the Universe, and as she had moved on from the effect to the cause her heart had filled with the True Beloved Who created and formed that magnificent work.

As for Joseph, on him be peace, with his matchless beauty that put the looking-glass to shame and dimmed the radiance of the sun, he was comparing Zulaykha's present plight with that erstwhile splendor of hers that used to cancel the light of the moon at the full, and made voluptuaries fall prostrate before her. Suddenly, pity welled up in him and, opening his hands to the Divine Unity, he begged his Lord to restore to Zulaykha her former youth and beauty. His prayer was answered, in accordance with the maxim:

The sign of love once gained,
The Beloved must be attained.

In an instant, Zulaykha recovered her old beauty, freshness, and charm. He took in marriage this woman who had suffered agony and torment all those years for love of him. He made Zulaykha achieve her desire. By marrying Zulaykha, he made a queen of this lady who, for love of him, had become a beggar.

And yet, as we mentioned above, Zulaykha had finally come to realize Whose lover she was, Whose lover it was right for her to be. In the mirror of Joseph she had seen the beauty of the Friend, and no longer needed Joseph. She had found the True Beloved; He was the aim; He was the goal.

Hear what Seza'i has to say:
What did you see in what passes away?
The Friend has shown his countenance
In the mirror burnished bright as day.

However, there is no access to this road by way of false love, because for false lovers this road is fraught with difficulty and hardship. Those who reach Real Love are not taken in by pretenders; they believe in no other. They sacrifice body and soul for the True Beloved. Those who dare to make this sacrifice will surely feast and revel in the dear one's company:

If you are the Loved One's lover,
Beware of falling for any other.
Plunge, like Abraham, into the flame;
In this rose garden it causes no pain.

For those who fall into the Fire for the sake of God's love, the Fire becomes a rose garden; their eyes see God; they die before they die.

Or rather, they do not die, but come to be. They are with the Life Everlasting:

> Pass the rest by and follow love, O heart;
> Reality's folk obey love, for their part.
> Love is more ancient than all known to exist:
> They sought love's beginning, but found it had no start.

The people of Reality say: "A sin committed with love is more meritorious than a loveless act of worship." For loveless worship is no more rewarded than a vain exertion. A sin committed with love will result in punishment, of course, but at least it is enjoyable. So whatever you do, do it with love! The venerable Suleyman Chelebi says, in that great and admired masterpiece of his, the *Mevlid-i Sherif:*

> Longingly the tongue but once the name of Allah breathes,
> And all one's sins come tumbling down like autumn leaves.

How true, how accurate! Instead of saying "Allah" one thousand times without love and longing, just say "Allah" once with love and longing—that is all you need. Many there be, very many indeed, who attain the Beloved by saying "Allah" just once with love and longing.

O wayfarer of Reality!

Three letters and five dots are what make the dervish a dervish. In Arabic, the word for Love is spelled with the three letters *'ayn, shin,* and *qaf* (عشق). There are three dots on the letter *shin* (ش) and two on the letter *qaf* (ق). The three letters and five dots that make the dervish a dervish are the Sovereign Power of Love. The loveless is no dervish, or at least none worthy of the name.

Yes, the dervish's stock-in-trade is Love. His knowledge is Love.

His experience is Love. His riding-mount is Love. His wishes and desires are Love. Those who do not drink the wine of "He loves them and they love Him" (Koran 5:54), who do not forsake themselves body and soul, who do not tread love's path bareheaded and barefoot, they cannot be dervishes. The dervish's life is Love, his darling is Love, his very self is Love—that is all there is to say!

> Unless you'd give your life for your beloved,
> You'd better not lay claim to being a lover.

God, Mighty and Glorious is He, is the lover of His dear one the Prophet; our master, God's dear one, is the lover of God, Exalted is He; the chief of God's lovers is our master, the beloved of the Almighty. All lovers are inheritors of that love, Majnuns of that love. The sun turns by that love, the moon by that longing, the stars by that example.

O dervish, calling yourself a lover!

With His love do you not whirl around? With His love do you not travel the eighteen thousand worlds? Then take the floor and whirl with His love, address Him with love, call on Him with love! As for the dervish who is a true lover, while his hand is at work, his heart is with his Beloved. Whatever job he does, whatever his business may be, it never distracts him from Remembrance of God. His eye is tearful with longing for the divine vision; his heart is seared by divine love. The eyes of the dervish who is a true lover see nought but God; his heart knows nought but Him. God is the eye by which he sees, the hand with which he holds, and the tongue with which he speaks.

The dervish is the "son of the moment"; he is ready to renounce renunciation. The dervish's litany is the illustrious name of Allah. The dervish does not stop at the names, but discovers the Named and surrenders to his Beloved. The dervish has no worries and no cares. His sole concern is God, his pain is God, his remedy is God, his cure is God, his cause is God. Were he not in love, he would pass away. If his heart should be devoid of love for as much as a single moment, the dervish could not stay alive. Love is the dervish's life, his health, his comfort. Love ruins the dervish, makes him weep; union makes him flourish, brings him to life. The dervish finds separation in union, union in separation.

Love makes us speak; love makes us moan; love makes us die; love brings us to life; love makes us drunk and bewildered; it sometimes makes one a king. Love and the lover have no rigid doctrine. Whichever direction the lover takes he turns toward his beloved. Wherever he may be, he is with his beloved. Wherever he goes, he goes with his beloved. He cannot do anything, cannot survive for one moment even, without his beloved. He constantly recalls his beloved, as his beloved remembers him. Lover and beloved, rememberer and remembered, are ever in each other's company, always together.

A person often remembers the object of his love. One who is a lover of God, Exalted is He, also remembers Him, always and everywhere. This is the duty and proof of love; this much does love demand. On the bough of the beloved's rosebush, love's nightingale sings its love incessantly.

Love brings the servant near to God, Glorified and Exalted is He. Love reminds the slave of his servitude and increases his devotion. Love removes vanity and hypocrisy, increases truthfulness and sincerity. Love solves all problems, opens all closed doors.

For love's sake the sky has been raised up and the earth has been spread out. For love's sake the universe has been created and adorned. Love makes us cross the deserts; love makes the traveling easy. Love overturns the mountains, smoothes out all obstacles. Love illumines the heart and delights the mind. Love causes neither sleep nor hunger nor thirst. Love makes us weep, love makes us speak, love makes us moan, love makes us hear. It is love that creates all the fine arts. Everything is brought into being and created for the sake of love. For love's sake wars are fought, eyes are filled with bloody tears. How many rosy faces have turned pale and faded because of love.

Love made Ferhad penetrate the mountains; it gave Majnun self-knowledge as he traversed the blazing, trackless wastes; it gave Wamiq a moment's respite as he crossed the seas. Love made the distant lover into the intimate lover. Love makes the shack on a lonely mountaintop into a palace; it turns many a splendid palace into a dungeon. Love brings the sultan to the slave's condition, the slave to that of the sultan. Love brings prosperity to lands pillaged by armies, and ruin to many a prosperous land. Love pours forth as poetry from the lover's mouth and rises up in monuments from his pen; it is planted as a slender sapling of love in the heart of each and every seeker. Love dragged Mansur to the gallows, fanned the fire in the heart of Mevlana, rendered Ibrahim Adham perplexed, and made Joseph the sovereign of Egypt.

The whole universe, being, and creation began with love; with love they should rightly end. Everything in the universe is doomed to pass away, but love is everlasting. The bearers of the Throne hold up the Throne with love. All the angels in the heavens congratulate one another in celebration of the Divine Love. Riding on love, the Almighty's dear friend passed by the Throne and went around the Divine Footstool. With love, the Lover brought His beloved to within "two bow-lengths." All the stairs of the Gardens of Paradise, adorned for love's sake, have been raised aloft with love.

In heaven—love; on earth—love; to the right—love; to the left—love; everywhere and everything is love. Love is He; the Lover is He; the Beloved is He; the Loved One is He; the Dear One is He; the Friend is He. The knight of love will reach his beloved early or late. He who gives his life for love will sooner or later find his dearest.

LOVE OF GOD

Love Him, that He may love you too. Unless He loves, you cannot love Him; unless He is seeking you, you cannot seek Him. Love your beloved, for the beloved is He; love your own true self, for your own true self is also He.

THE CHEST IN THE ROOM

4

REMEMBRANCE

O sincere lover!

The shortest route by which to draw near to God is Remembrance, *dhikr*. The chief of the two worlds, the beloved of the All-Merciful, the leader of lovers, the guide of the sincere, and the Messenger of the end of time told the prince of men, the bearer of the secret of the Koran, our master Imam 'Ali, may God ennoble his countenance and be pleased with him, that by way of dhikr—and dhikr alone—would it be possible to attain Divine Approval. He clearly explained and related the various kinds of dhikr and how each one was or should be. According to these descriptions we distinguish seven categories of dhikr:

I . Public (audible) dhikr
2. Private (secret) dhikr
3. Dhikr of the heart
4. Dhikr of the spirit
S. Dhikr of the mystery of the spirit
6. Dhikr of the mystery of the inmost heart
7. Dhikr of the mystery of the mystery

It is only the saints, lovers, and believers who thus—and very, very often—remember the Lord Most High. The hypocrites very seldom remember God, Exalted is He, because they are doubting, and because their mouths and hearts are not in unison. As for the unbelievers, they are in darkness and in prison because they have turned their faces away from Divine Remembrance. The earthly lives of those who turn their faces away from Divine Remembrance will surely remain in darkness, their breasts will be oppressed with heartache and woes, and their deaths will be very difficult and distressing. The likes of these will face severe torment in the grave and in the interval between death and Judgment; they will be raised from their graves and resurrected blind. This blindness of theirs will drag them down to the fire of Hell. They will weep and groan imploringly:

"O Lord! During our life on earth we had eyes and could see. Now You have resurrected us blind: What is the cause and inner meaning of this?"

And the Almighty will reply:

"You did not remember Me during your Life on earth and you turned your faces from remembrance of Me as long as you lived. The penalty for turning the face from My remembrance is to be resurrected blind—the fate you have suffered this day."

Moreover, although the eyes of those who do not remember and glorify Almighty God in this world are not unseeing, such people are in truth and in reality blind. It must be well understood that seeing does not mean seeing only with the eyes in your head. What good is to be expected of those who can see with the eyes in their heads, if the eyes of their hearts are blind and they cannot see truth and reality? Will not the soil sooner or later fill in the place of the eye in the head? God, Mighty and Glorious is He, has clearly and explicitly declared and announced in His Koran, the Decisive Proof, that those in whom the eye of the heart is blind in this transient world will be blind in the eternal world as well.

This being the case, the Remembrance of God is the eye's light and the heart's delight. It is the luster of hearts and the solace of minds. It is the shortest route to God, Exalted is He. Those happy and fortunate souls who achieve the grace and favor of remembering His illustrious Names are the lovers of God, who converse with God, Exalted is He, and enjoy His loving company.

This blessing is unattainable for those who do not love God, Exalted is He, and for those whom God, Exalted is He, does not love; they are therefore unable to remember the Truth. Those who wish to love God, Exalted is He, and to be worthy of His love, who desire to be annihilated in the Truth and to be with the Truth eternally, must remember God constantly. Those who want to be beloved of the True Beloved must always and everywhere remember and extol Him, and must thus disclose their love and affection for Him. Just as all the Messengers have told us quite plainly that through dhikr—and dhikr alone—can this great blessing be achieved, and that through dhikr—and dhikr alone—is it possible to meet with God, Exalted is He, the same message has been announced and proclaimed to all mankind by the beloved of God, Exalted is He, the Almighty's dear friend, to him and his family the most excellent salutations, our revered master, who was graciously vouchsafed the honor and distinction of being called by the names RA'UF, RAHIM, and AZIZ, which are among the Divine Names.

The lover should remember God by whichever Names and in whichever manner he finds pleasing and delightful. When the lover remembers his Beloved, that is, when he declares his love to Him, it is certain that the Beloved will also be that lover's Lover. For this reason, it is permissible to remember God, Exalted is He, either openly or in secret, either in company or on one's own. Therefore, whatever Names and whatever mode the lover may find pleasing and delightful, such is the lover's proper disposition, and the Name he chooses for his dhikr is the Greatest Name.

The venerable Bayzid Bistami, sanctified be his lofty spirit, was asked: "Which of the Divine Names is the Greatest Name?"

To this he replied: "Which of the Names of God, Exalted is He, is the least, that you should ask me which of them is the Greatest?"

Yes, each of the Divine Names is the Greatest Name. Whichever of these Names is appropriate for the remembering lover, that is the Greatest Name for that lover. For instance, for our master the venerable Imam 'Ali, may God ennoble his countenance and be pleased with him, the Greatest Name was the pair of Names HAYY and QAYYUM. For our lady Aisha, may God be pleased with her and with her father, the Greatest Name was YA RABB. As for the venerable Abu Bakr the Truthful, may God be pleased with him, he preferred WAHID, RAHMAN, and RAHIM.

Let me repeat and stress emphatically:

There is no "smallest" Name of God, Exalted is He: All His illustrious Names are equally beautiful, high, and great. You can compare this with the examples we have given above. According to the knower of the Divine Mysteries, the noble Muhyiddin ibn 'Arabi, may God sanctify his spirit:

"The lover may remember God, Exalted is He, by those of His Names he prefers."

There are many verses in the Koran, as well as noble traditions in the Prophetic Hadith, concerning the Remembrance of God. All these revered verses and noble traditions decree and prescribe for us the necessity of remembering God, Exalted is He, very, very much and very, very often.

Some narrow-minded people have expressed the grossly mistaken view that outspoken dhikr is impermissible. As is well known, it is beyond doubt or uncertainty that the greatest dhikr in Islam is the prescribed ritual prayer. In three out of the five daily prayers, the recitation is pronounced aloud. To these can be added the Friday prayer in congregation and the two festival prayers. Moreover, the recitations of ALLAHU AKBAR at the Feast of Sacrifice, of LABBAYK at Arafat, and of ALLAHU AKBAR on setting out from home and going to the noble mosque at the Feasts of Ramadan and Sacrifice, all are pronounced in an audible voice. So it is commanded, and it is natural and obvious that no one has sufficient power to alter this. What greater proof and evidence could there be, therefore, for the permissibility of public dhikr?

In battles with the enemies of God, the open expression of His remembrance is required by the illustrious command of the Messenger. In the face of so much that is explicit and obvious, who would dare to come out and say that outspoken dhikr is not permissible? Who could find it in him to make so bold a statement?

It is well known to all scholars and men of faith that our master, the Glory of the Universe, God bless him and give him peace, taught private dhikr to Abu Bakr the truthful, may God be pleased with him, when they were hiding in a cave from their pursuing foes during their migration, Hijra, to Medina the Illuminated. Someone pursued by his enemies and hiding in a cave would most certainly not be able to do public dhikr. Were he to do so, he would run a dangerous risk of betraying his whereabouts to his pursuers.

This action of the glorious Messenger clearly informs us, therefore, that private dhikr is permissible.

The honorable commentators are unanimously agreed in assigning to the period before the Hijra the revelation of the noble verse of the Koran of which the exalted meaning is: "Make your remembrance, your entreaty, and your supplication of your Lord in secret." Before the Hijra, if the believers did their dhikr and their prayer openly, they exposed themselves to the aggression and molestation of the polytheists. For this reason, the prayer was performed audibly at three of the prescribed times (namely dawn, sunset, and bedtime), when the unbelievers had withdrawn to their houses. While performing the noon and afternoon prayers, the polytheists being out and about the streets at those hours, they did their recitation privately. As for the Call to Prayer instituted by Muhammad, on him be peace, the fact of its having become established practice only after the Hijra provides decisive evidence in support and confirmation of this view of ours.

In other words, before the Hijra the Divine Remembrance was performed privately—secretly, that is to say—owing to the very real necessity of avoiding the cruel torment, aggression, and molestation of the polytheists. Even today, private dhikr is compulsory under certain conditions. In countries governed by Marxist and materialist regimes, the believers perform their obligatory prayers in secret so as to avoid the aggression of the irreligious, reciting the obligatory Koranic readings covertly not only in the noon and afternoon prayers, but also in those of dawn, sunset, and bedtime.

If we consider the matter fairly and perceptively, we come to the conclusion that there is no objection to reciting the Remembrance of God either secretly or openly. We understand that there is no obstacle to either in religious law. This is a form of worship that is left entirely to the pleasure of the one performing the Remembrance of God. The lover who is enraptured by private dhikr will attain the abode of his desire by remembering God, Exalted is He, in secret. He who delights in public dhikr will openly remember the Almighty. We humbly pray, in all simplicity and sincerity, that all lovers may attain their abode and destination.

Our master, the protector of the Divine Law, most perfect salutations to him and his family, said to his noble companions:

"When your path leads you into the garden of Paradise, eat of the fruit of those gardens. Gather the roses of those gardens and smell their scent!"

When they asked: "What is the garden of Paradise, O Messenger of God?" the chief of the two worlds gave this felicitous reply:

"The circle of the dhikr is the garden of Paradise!"

With the rocks and mountains high,
Let me call, my Lord, on Thee.
At the dawn with birds that fly,
Let me call, my Lord, on Thee.

With the fish beneath the sea,
At the dawn, with "Woe is me!"
Crazy with the cry "O He!"
Let me call, my Lord, on Thee.

With Jesus on high,
With Moses on Mount Sinai,
With the rod that he holds by,
Let me call, my Lord, on Thee.

With Job in all his suffering drear,
With Jacob shedding many a tear,
With Muhammad, loved so dear,
Let me call, my Lord, on Thee.

With thankful praise addressed to God,
With the Koran's "Say: He is God,"
With bare feet, with head uncovered,
Let me call, my Lord, on Thee.

With this song Yunus regales,
Singing with the nightingales,
With the Truth's most loving slaves,
Let me call, my Lord, on Thee.

The happy and fortunate participants in the circle of the dhikr may remember God, Exalted is He, either in secret or openly. But if they make their remembrance in secret, will anyone watching that circle be able to comprehend what they are doing? In other words, it is public dhikr that is required when the dhikr is performed in the circle. Those who see, hear, and understand this public dhikr will be able to join that assembly. Indeed, the dhikr recommended by the glorious Messenger, and likened by him to the garden of Paradise, is dhikr performed publicly. It is agreed, then, that even in the Prophet's own blessed time lovers used to sit in the dhikr circle and remember God, Exalted is He. It is as clear as day that the Prophet of the end of time summoned his companions and his Community to the Remembrance of God by these noble sayings of his. The fact that he did not forbid public dhikr, but on the contrary encouraged and approved it, definitely establishes the permissibility of remembering God, Exalted is He, openly.

Noticing that a detachment he had sent out toward the enemy was doing dhikr in a loud voice, the Prophet stopped them with the words: "Almighty God is not far away, nor is He deaf." But his purpose here was to prevent the foe from being alerted by the audible dhikr and so barring their escape, or from taking precautionary measures in readiness to face the believers.

It is true that the founder of our school of Islamic law, the Great Imam Abu Hanifa, may God have mercy upon him, reasoned that public dhikr was disapproved. However, men of learning are agreed that even a great jurist, *mujtahid,* is capable of error. For *mujtahids* get two rewards when they are correct in their jurisprudential reasoning, while if they are mistaken they still deserve one reward. It may be supposed that, in forming this opinion of his, the venerable Imam was swayed by feelings of compassion for the Community of Muhammad. God knows best, but another possible reason for this kind of judgment might be to preserve the Community of Muhammad from hypocritical ostentation.

As for the Two Imams (Abu Hanifa's great disciples, Abu Yusuf and Muhammad Shaybani), public dhikr is permissible according to them. Practice is based on these juristic opinions in accordance with the place, the moment, the person, and the time. The individual needs to know where a "Yes!" is in order and where a "No!" is called for. One who does not know where, when, and how to act, nor what he ought to do, is negligent of his duty. The awareness and perceptivity of those whose intelligence, conscience, and common sense are in the right place are demonstrated by their measured caution at every step. For a person sought and pursued by his enemies, to give a loud cry of "Allah" would likely be the death of him. It would be insane in the circumstances.

O my brother, desiring the Divine Love and seeking after Reality!

It is not right to embark haphazardly and with half-baked knowledge upon the attempt to explain and interpret the noble Traditions. As is well known, it is necessary to know the context in which they arose. It is very important to establish and determine precisely whether noble Hadith transmitted by God's Messenger, God bless him and give him peace, belong to the period before or to that following the Hijra. They may have been transmitted in peace at home, on a journey, in time of war, at night, during the day, in winter, in summer, to one person, or to a group. All these factors must be taken properly into account. The science of Hadith is a thoroughgoing branch of knowledge. It is therefore possible, indeed probable, that those who are not properly versed and qualified in the science of Hadith will fall into error when expounding and interpreting the noble Traditions. This was sternly forbidden by our master, the Glory of the Universe, God bless him and give him peace.

It is categorically stated in a noble Hadith that a dwelling place in Hell has been prepared for those who dare to pretend that the Messenger said what God did not say, or who have the effrontery to impute falsehood to him; certain heedless and ignorant persons have been admonished with the reminder that the Community of Muhammad needs to be extremely wary of this. Consequently, the wisest course is to consult those learned in Hadith on all matters pertaining to the noble Traditions.

It is likewise certain and inevitable that those will perish who presume to interpret the meaning of the Noble Koran and its illustrious verses on the basis of their personal and subjective ideas, without reference to the accepted and reputable commentaries.

We seek refuge from both situations with God, Exalted is He.

O seeker of the Truth!

We have already explained that the permissibility of public dhikr has been firmly established by the judgment of the Two Imams. Official legal pronouncements on this question also follow the opinion of the Two Imams. As for the founders of the other schools of Islamic Law, the venerable Imams Shafi'i, Ahmad ibn Hanbal, and Malik ibn Anas, may God have mercy on them all, as well as the other great *mujtahids* and honorable jurists, although their knowledge of jurisprudence has led them to formulate opinions on many other subjects (sometimes with hairsplitting subtlety), they have not reached any definite conclusion regarding the Remembrance of God. They have given no pronouncements on how the Remembrance of God should be performed, leaving this matter to the lover's own taste. Nevertheless, they have issued pronouncements stating the penalties to be imposed upon those envious, spiteful bigots who oppose the Remembrance of God and declare whirling to be impermissible, thereby seeking to prohibit and deny the practices of the saints of God.

Those who wish to get some idea of the nature and contents of these pronouncements must take as indispensable reading the *Rulings of 'Umar* and the authoritative works comprising the legal rulings issued by the commentator and Sheikh ul-Islam, Ebu-Su'ud Efendi, and Zenbilli Ali Jemali Efendi.

The permissible character of whirling is established by noble Koranic verse. In His Koran, the Decisive Proof, God, Mighty and Glorious is He, praises those who remember the Essence of His Divinity while standing, while sitting, and when lying on their sides, for He orders and commands us to mention His Illustrious Name in every state and action. It is certain that, on the strength of this verse, Remembrance of God has all along been performed *qiyaman* (while standing) and that whirling dates from the time of the Successors. In accordance with the words of the Almighty's dear friend: "After my own time, the best time is the time of the Successors," standing dhikr and whirling have been performed from that time on by the people of God and—may God be pleased with them all—none of the scholars who have come and gone has prevented this. Quite the contrary; rulings have been given pronouncing it lawful, and lovers have not only been permitted to whirl, but positively urged and encouraged to do so. Thanks to all this, millions of Sufis and Lovers through the centuries, each occupying an honorable and distinguished position in the world of Islam, have continued to practice standing dhikr and whirling.

As with the whirling validated by the noble Koranic verse, the exalted meaning of which we cited above, it is possible to adduce clear verses to establish and confirm the circumambulation and whirling of the Angels nigh to God around the Divine Throne, as well as the circumambulation and turning around the Revered Kaaba performed by millions of Muslims every year. The people of Reality are well aware that whirling is actually done to symbolize these. The whirling of lovers is the medicine of their hearts.

According to the celebrated work called *Zad ul-Ma'ad,* the permissibility of musical dhikr, *sama',* and whirling is proven by the fact that the Almighty's dear friend did *sama'* with his noble Companions, and that when one of the Companions exclaimed on seeing this: "O Messenger of God! What a fine dance you have there," he said: "Hush! Hush! This is no dance—it is Remembrance of the Love of the Friend."*

As is also well known, it is true that the tambourine *(mazhar)* and cymbals *(halile)* are used during the musical and whirling dhikr. It is known for a fact that these musical instruments, rashly described as playthings by certain careless people, were used in the Prophet's own blessed time. When the Almighty's dear friend went to Medina the Illumined, the noble Helpers greeted him by striking the tambourine and chanting odes, and the Chief of the two worlds did not forbid this ceremony of welcome. Moreover, it is also a fact

*Confirmation and corroboration of this view is to be found in the treatise on *sama'* in the *Ihya 'Ulumiddin* of Hujjat ul-Islam Imam al-Ghazali.

that he said to Abu Bakr the Truthful, may God be pleased with him, as the latter was about to put a stop to the beating of tambourines and chanting of odes one feast day in the Abode of Bliss and in the Prophetic Presence:

"O son of Qahafa! Every nation and every people has its own festival. Today is their festival, so let them make music and sing."

Since the festivals and hijras of Sufis and lovers take place during their dhikr, it has been permitted for centuries and the idea of preventing it never crossed anyone's mind.

Yes, the festivals of Sufis and lovers are the moment when they remember God, Exalted is He. Since God also remembers one who remembers His Essence of Divinity, the dhikr is the union of servant with God, the festival of lovers. Besides, since the Voyage to God takes place in the dhikr, there is also a hijra for lovers through Remembrance of God. This is why Sufis beat the tambourine during their whirling.

Is it not by the drum, a larger version of the tambourine beaten during the *sama'* and whirling, that we are awakened for the final meal before the Fast which we observe as one of the five pillars of Islam? In battles waged for the supremacy of God's word against the enemies of the faith, are not maces beaten when an assault is made with the intention of discharging the religious duty of Jihad? Are not battle hymns chanted, while the military band plays stirring marches to encourage the warriors of Islam? Are not maces, drums, and cymbals beaten as the Koran-reciters chant at the top of their voices: "Help from God and victory near"? In other words, these things are necessary, essential, prerequisite even, to the performance of certain acts of worship and to some obligatory religious duties in particular. Since the Remembrance of God, like Fasting and Jihad, is warfare with Satan and his forces, it is quite definitely lawful for this Sufi warfare to be waged with tambourine, cymbals, flute, and drum. Great men of learning and rectitude have given many legal rulings to this effect.

It is consequently quite wrong of those who witness dhikr, whirling, and *sama'* to accuse the dervishes of "playing games, dancing, and making frivolous music," and those who take action against them are guilty of grievous sin. It should never be lost from sight that they will see the results of this sin in their lives.

O seeker of the Truth!

For those who wish to love God, Exalted is He, to be worthy of the love of God, Exalted is He, to be with the Truth eternally through annihilation in Him; for those whose desire it is to be favored with the love of the True Beloved, to enjoy mutual affection, intimacy, and togetherness with Him, and to achieve all these blessings, it is absolutely necessary to embark upon the way of love. They must grasp the hand of one who knows God. Hand in hand is hand in hand with God. The Almighty's dear friend informs us that Divine Remembrance alone is the one and only way to reach this blessing and success. The Prince of Sainthood, the venerable Imam 'Ali, may God ennoble his countenance and be pleased with him, one day asked the Almighty's dear friend, the Glory of the two worlds and Mercy to mankind:

"O Messenger of God! What is the shortest way by which to reach God, Exalted is He?"

Our master, the Chief of Messengers, vouchsafed this felicitous reply:

"O 'Ali! The shortest way by which to reach God, Exalted is He, is Divine Remembrance. The most excellent dhikr, which opens the gates of Paradise, closes the doors of Hell, and transforms fire into light, is the confession and affirmation of that saving declaration of the Oneness of God: LA ILAHA ILLA-LLAH."

All the Messengers were sent by God, the Lord of Majesty and Perfection, in order to inculcate and teach this exalted formula. This lofty expression is the essence of the One Hundred Sacred Writings, and the meaning of the Four Books of Scripture. The Throne, the Footstool, the Tablet, the Pen, the Great Lotus Tree, heaven and earth and all intermediate worlds, visible and invisible, known or unknown—all have been created and brought into being for the sake of this exalted declaration.

This lofty declaration brings forth God's Mercy overflowing. Thanks to this Good Word, the whole universe enjoys the favor of Divine Mercy. Sinners are pardoned and forgiven by virtue of this exalted formula. Atheists and hypocrites, too, are able to find a bite of bread and a drop of water in honor of this declaration. This blessed expression is the prop of the Throne and the support of the Footstool. The waves of the sea, the winds and the storms, the birds that fly in the sky, the nightingales trilling on the rose bough, the ships that plow the deep, airplanes that take off into the heavens, all metals and machines—everything, but everything, declares and repeats that exalted confession, each thing singing its natural tune.

The universe is a mighty *dergah:** Sun, moon, and stars are the brightly shining lamps of this *dergah.* The dervishes of this *dergah* are the entirety of beings, while those who do dhikr there are all the creatures that exist. That Scent comes from the rose. That Cry is heard from the lover. The nightingales are singing for the Master of that Word. Unknowing and even unawares, the unbelievers are confessing Him in spite of their denial; unknowing and unawares they are remembering Him. He is everywhere, and everything is He. He has created everything, and everything He has encompassed. There is nought but He; there is only He. And it is He Who will exist forever. He has no beginning; He is the First of the first, the Last of the last. The outer is He; the inner is He. All-Powerful is He; in all directions everything visible or invisible is He. Everywhere and in everything His matchless power, His incomparable handiwork, show forth. He is living and enduring. In everything and everywhere He is everlasting.

**Dergah:* Meeting place where dhikr is performed.

5

THE AFFIRMATION OF UNITY

O Lover!

So, LA ILAHA ILLA-LLAH (There is no god but God) was His Name. The ways and means of passing beyond the Name to reach the One Named had also been demonstrated. This was possible only through dhikr, remembering Him. LA ILAHA ILLA-LLAH was His favorite Name. He would unfailingly answer anyone who called Him by this Name, and would not turn away empty-handed anyone who remembered Him by this Name. That is why lovers and devotees would chorus LA ILAHA ILLA-LLAH with every breath.

To this very day, lovers and devotees continue to proclaim the Divine Unity: LA ILAHA ILLA-LLAH. Until the day of Resurrection and Judgment, as long as there is a single true believer left on the face of the earth, LA ILAHA ILLA-LLAH will go on being repeated.

For this Name topples mountains; this Name turns darkness into light. This Name makes the wretched happy. This Name dispels all evils. This Name cleanses tarnished hearts. This Name brings the lover to the Beloved. This Name ends all difficulties. This Name brings man together with the Truth. This Name makes a man faithful to his promise. This Name is the remedy for all ills, the healer of incurable wounds. This Name brings tears to the lover's eyes. This Name is the undoing of disbelievers and hypocrites. This Name makes those who are weeping smile. This Name brings the traveler to his destination. The names of lover and Beloved are united in this Name, and through this union is revealed the secret of the glorious verse: "Till he was but two bow-lengths off" (Koran 53:9).

Do we not mention very, very often the one we love? We do this not from any fear of forgetting the loved one, but because we wish in this way to proclaim our love. Is it likely or even possible that anyone seriously and genuinely in love should forget the beloved? Of course not. Thus our remembrance of God, Exalted is He, is a kind of declaration and proclamation of our love for Him. That is why lovers always, everywhere, and at every opportunity remember Him. The more they remember Him, the more their love and affection grow; every remembrance adds love to their love. If man, a mere creature, is unable to forget the one he loves, could God, the Lord of Majesty and Perfection, forget His creature, when He is utterly free and devoid of all forgetfulness and heedlessness? Will He not remember him as He has promised? Indeed, just as He links with the declaration of His Unity the remembrance of His beloved Prophet, plainly announcing and explaining that for love of him He created and brought into being this whole universe, so He will certainly not forget and will love all of His creatures who remember Him; He will remember His servant.

We have convincing evidence of this in the many practical examples we witness in our daily lives. If a person loves someone with the ordinary metaphorical kind of love, he will never stop talking about his loved one; he will raise the subject at every opportunity and on any pretext, mentioning the loved one's name and speaking of nothing else. Indeed, he will not be content with doing this just by himself, but will wish and even expect his listeners to do the same. With his beloved's name on his lips, his beloved's image before his eyes, the flame of his love for the beloved blazing in his heart, he remembers her constantly, believing that each time he does so he draws a little closer to his loved one and thinking that one day she will come to love him too. He is therefore filled with yearning and longing to behold his loved one, in his dreams at night and with his ordinary eyes by day.

Then how could those who love God, Exalted is He, with Real Love and who in turn are loved by Him, how could they forsake remembrance of their Beloved? The Name of Allah is the very life of the Lover, the proof of his faith. This Blessed Name of the Sultan of sultans is LA ILAHA ILLA-LLAH. The glorious Divine Name is the stronghold of God, Exalted is He, the summit of His beacon light, and the highest of all the Names by which He is remembered. Those who mention His Name, their hearts become pure light, their breasts are filled with joy, their efforts are gratefully accepted, their sins are all forgiven. Whenever the Divine Name is uttered, one ought to follow the assertion of Divine Unity—LA ILAHA ILLA-LLAH—by pronouncing the noble sentence MUHAMMADUN RASULU-LLAH (Muhammad is God's Messenger). If this is not pronounced aloud, it should always be felt inwardly after each declaration of the Divine Unity, the benefit and blessing from which will then be promptly received.

The lovers of God derive their strength and spiritual energy from dhikr. They find happiness and glory in this world and in the Hereafter. For lovers of God, remembrance of Him is like breathing air or drinking water. Just as no one can live without taking breath or drinking water, it is impossible and inconceivable that the lovers of God should be able to exist without remembering God Almighty. Those who do remember God, Exalted is He, can see the countenance of the Truth in this world, becoming happy and cheerful, finding peace and repose. In contrast, those who cannot see the Truth in this world will not be able to see the Truth in the world of eternity. In neither world can they rub their faces in the footsteps of the Messenger. It is impossible to imagine anyone less fortunate than those who cannot experience rubbing in their eyes the dust from the blessed feet of God's Beloved Prophet.

The following anecdote should summarize and distill the essence of everything we have tried to explain above, in order to inculcate this affection, to instruct the Community of Muhammad in this way of love.

As we mentioned earlier on, our master the venerable Imam 'Ali, may God ennoble his countenance and be pleased with him, once appeared in the presence of the radiant majesty of the Messenger and asked:

"O Messenger of God, would you kindly tell me which is the nearest road by which to reach God, Exalted and Sanctified is He, and which is the most meritorious in the sight of God, glorious is His Majesty, and the easiest for us creatures?"

The Prince of the two worlds, who is "Mercy to the universe," vouchsafed this felicitous reply:

"O 'Ali, it is that blessed, saving sentence, the cause of the manifestation of my Prophethood. Continue to utter that sacred sentence."

"What is that sacred sentence, O Messenger of God?"

"It is your continuous declaration of the Divine Unity, and remembrance of God in solitude and wherever you are and whatever you may be doing."

"Is the merit of remembrance comparable to that of the laws you have been bidden to propagate? For all the faithful—praise be to Allah—do remember God, Exalted is He."

"O 'Ali, know this well: As long as there is anyone on earth saying 'Allah, Allah . . . ' the Resurrection will not begin."

"O Messenger of God, how should I remember my Lord?"

"O 'Ali, close your eyes and be still! Let me make remembrance thrice, while you listen and hear it from me; then you make remembrance thrice while I listen."

Having said this, our master the King of the Prophetic Mission closed his blessed eyes and repeated three times the glorious Name, the affirmation of Divine Unity: LA ILAHA ILLA-LLAH, which is the best remembrance. In so doing, he pronounced LA ILAHA to the right and then, turning his blessed head to the left, toward his enlightened heart, he completed his utterance with ILLA-LLAH. With his blessed eyes closed, he pronounced the remembrance of the Divine Unity in an audible voice.

When the Prince of the two worlds had completed the remembrance in this manner, the Sovereign of sainthood, our master Imam 'Ali, repeated three times the remembrance of Divine Unity, as he had seen and learned it from him. Closing his eyes, he said LA ILAHA to his right, then ILLA-LLAH to his left. This time God's Messenger, God bless and give him peace, watched the remembrance being performed by the venerable Imam 'Ali just as he had done it himself. After he had performed the remembrance just as he had seen it taught by the Beloved Prophet, his noble heart, already polished and purified by love of Muhammad, became light—light upon light. In other words, he made the mirror of his heart shine with the polish of the affirmation of Divine Unity, attained perfect bliss, and witnessed many strange secrets and divine mysteries. For he had drunk the wine of Unity from the blessed hands of the most holy person, the noblest of all creatures, and had transcended himself. Having attained and witnessed the bounty and blessing of the beloved Messenger, he had become heir to the Prophetic wisdom, the gate to the city of true knowledge, the Sovereign of Sainthood, and the cup-bearer of the Waters of Paradise.

The heirs of our master the venerable Imam 'Ali, may God ennoble his countenance and be pleased with him, are the saints—those fortunate and happy beings, who rejoice outwardly in the light of the illustrious Sacred Law of Islam and inwardly in the secrets of its noble rules; as inheritors of the Prophets and of the Sovereign of men, they have revived many a dead heart with the radiance of

Unity and enabled it to witness the divine mysteries. With one glance of their eyes full of kindness and compassion, they have granted many lovers direct vision and the attainment of their desire. They have brought them, sometimes objectively, sometimes subjectively, both spiritually and physically, to visit the worlds of the Angelic Realm and the Realm of Dominion, enabling them to orbit the world of Divinity, and letting them approach the universe of the Reality of Realities. Lovers who read the lives of the Intimates of God will vouch for the validity of these statements.

The abode where all mystical paths arise and become manifest is the Divine Abode, the presence of God Himself, Lord of majesty and perfection. Our Exalted Lord, All-Powerful and All-Glorious, taught the remembrance of Divine Unity to Gabriel, on him be peace, who taught it in turn to the beloved Prophet.

As we have already pointed out, it was in the cave where they were hiding in the course of their migration from Mecca the Ennobled to Medina the Illumined, that our master the Sultan of the Prophets, the most excellent salutations to him and his family, instructed the venerable Abu Bakr the Veracious, may God be pleased with him, in private dhikr.

Audible dhikr was taught to the venerable Imam 'Ali, may God ennoble his countenance and be pleased with him, in the manner we have just explained. Imam 'Ali taught it to his two sons, the venerable Imams Hasan and Hussein, may God be pleased with them all. Still later, it was taught to the venerable Hasan al-Basri and Kumayyil ibn Zayyad, may God be pleased with them both. Then Hasan al-Basri taught Habib al-A'jam; Habib al-A'jam taught Da'ud al-Ta'i; Da'ud al-Ta'i taught Sari al-Saqati; then Sari al-Saqati taught his sister's son, that is his nephew, the preeminent Junayd al-Baghdadi. To be more explicit, those who performed the audible dhikr, and so transmitted the breath of Muhammad, were the heads of all the Sufi orders, and in this way they have bestowed the Divine Love upon lovers until the Day of Resurrection.

As a branch of the Khalwatiya,* our order comes down from the venerable Hasan al-Basri. Public dhikr is performed by the orders of all the blessed Sheikhs whose names we have mentioned above. All branches of these orders are descended from the four great chiefs as successors of the venerable Imam 'Ali, may God ennoble his countenance and be pleased with him, and all of them practice public dhikr. The Qadiriya, Badawiya, Dussuqiya, Shadhiliya, Sa'diya, Maghribiya, Mawlawiya, Bektashiya, Khalwatiya, Jalwatiya, Arusiya, and all branches of these orders remember God, Exalted is He, by public dhikr.

However, the Naqshbandiya, the Way of our master the venerable Abu Bakr, the Veracious, may God be pleased with him, has divided into two sections. One section remembers God, Lord of majesty and perfection, and affirms His Unity with private dhikr, the other with public dhikr.

Of all acts performed for the sake of the noble pleasure of God, Exalted is He, the best and most beautiful is the affirmation of the Divine Unity. Decisive proof of its being the highest and greatest act is the noble Koranic verse: “But remembrance of God is greater” (29:45). Those blessed with insight and faith, who see Truth and reality, can deduce from this noble verse the loftiness of remembrance of God and its merit in God's sight, Exalted is He.

Our master, the Chief of Mankind and the Intercessor on the Day of Resurrection, said:

“The remembrance of God is the response to good tidings.”

To affirm the Divine Unity, whether openly or in secret, is required by command of the Lord and His sublime decree:

“Remember Me and I will remember you.”

It is sacred duty that every creature is obliged to fulfill. As the first of the fifty-four compulsory religious duties with which all believers are charged, the greatest and most meritorious of all acts of worship

*Translator's note: In Turkish, Halveti.

is to know God, Glorified and Exalted is He, to affirm His Oneness, to declare His Unity, and to remember Almighty God in every state and activity, to remember and glorify our One Lord always, everywhere, and at every opportunity.

The attempt to denigrate public dhikr on the grounds that it is "nothing but hypocritical ostentation" is not an act of genuine faith. God's Messenger, God bless him and give him peace, says in a noble Hadith:

"Remember God often—Exalted is He—even if the hypocrites call you impostors."

Does not the Prince of the two worlds mean to explain by this noble Hadith that, when they accuse those who publicly remember God, Glorified and Exalted is He, they are in fact hypocrites themselves?

O seeker after Truth!

It is permissible to make remembrance of Almighty God always and everywhere, at every opportunity and under any pretext. It is considered impermissible on two occasions only. The first of these is during sexual intercourse, and the other during the elimination of waste from the body. However, even these restrictions do not apply to the Intimates of God, whose hearts have a life of their own. These do not make their remembrance of their own desire and volition. It is their hearts that remember. For Intimates of the Truth who have attained this high degree, no condition or place is an obstacle to remembrance.

God, Magnified and Glorified is He, may be remembered while one is standing, sitting, lying on one's side, or even lying on one's back. It is permissible to remember Him in a noble mosque, in a church, in a synagogue—in short, in any place that is clean. For only the believers remember. Those who love God, Exalted is He, and who give their hearts to His beloved Prophet Muhammad Mustafa, God bless him and give him peace, take delight in the Divine Remembrance.

6

THE BELIEVERS AND THE UNBELIEVERS

O faithful lover, seeker on the path of Truth, wishing to remember God!

Both the merciful side and the wrathful aspect of God, Lord of Majesty and Perfection, exist in this world. Our Lord has hidden His good pleasure and His mercy among our good deeds, and His anger among our sinful acts. Yet He sometimes conceals His mercy within our sin, and His anger within our worship. For He is the Omnipotent, Who alone has the power to bring the dead to life and the living to death.

God, Magnified and Glorified is He, has made Remembrance of God the highest, loftiest, and most sublime of all beautiful acts. He has explained and extolled this truth, in His Mighty Proof the Koran and in the Traditions of His Great Messenger, as a divine gift and bounty for grateful servants and lovers who remember the Essence of Divinity. By explaining the meaning of Divine Remembrance, the relationship of those who remember to the One Remembered, and the high degrees attained by them, He has encouraged us, His creatures, and made us eager for Remembrance of God.

The Remembrance is the Name of Allah. The rememberer is the one who remembers God, Exalted is He. The One Remembered acts as a mutual remembrance, binding the one who remembers to the One Who is remembered. However, it is a condition for those who are lovers of God, Exalted is He, that they be in uprightness. They must guard hand, tongue, and loins from every act forbidden by their beloved Lord the Creator, and censured by the tongue of His beloved Prophet. Each one should obey the Beloved and fulfill the demands of this obedience with affection, sincerity, and purity. Since one should be able to sacrifice everything for the sake of the Beloved and for love of Him, one ought to be very wary and careful to avoid everything displeasing to Him. One should perform in love and gratitude everything He wishes to have done, taking great care for fear of hurting, saddening, or offending the Beloved. One should take the strictest precaution against displeasing the Lord through things He does not want done. Should it be one's fate somehow to incur the wrath of the Beloved, one should immediately seek His pardon, weep and sob with regret, repent and beg for forgiveness. You should know that so to beg pardon and forgiveness and so to repent are a hallmark of love and lover; in all awareness and consciousness you should remain sincere in your repentance.

All acts of worship and remembrance should be performed not in any hope of benefit, but with pure intention only to obtain the good pleasure of the Beloved. It is necessary to be in a state of absolute devotion and uprightness. For instance, acts of worship and remembrance performed for the sake of obtaining miraculous powers are of no value and cannot be accepted. Genuine lovers should be most careful to avoid this kind of thing. It may be a miracle to float on water, or to stay below water for a long period without breathing, but it should not be forgotten that these movements are natural to fish, while any vessel made of wood can make its way over water. It may be a miracle to fly in the air, but do not forget that birds and airplanes can make long journeys through the empty air. If it be a miracle to traverse space from one end of the world to the other, the devil and the jinn can perform this feat with the greatest of ease.

Anyway, do you consider miraculous the invention and use of electricity, telephone, or television, each of them a marvel of science?

God, Magnified and Glorified is He, does not want miracles from human beings. He does not expect the extraordinary. What he demands is respectful, affectionate, and upright worship of the Essence of Divinity, the fulfillment of a servant's duties. This is why he sent one hundred Tablets and four great Books, stating explicitly in every one of them His glorious divine decree:

"We created man and jinn only to worship Us."

Yes, Almighty God requires and expects from human beings affection, devotion, and uprightness toward the Essence of Divinity. This He has clearly explained in the one hundred Tablets and the four great Books. Miracles and feats cannot ensure this affection and uprightness, yet the crown of miracles may certainly one day be set upon the heads of loving and upright servants.

Lovers should be extremely careful to avoid unlawful things and should not touch anything displeasing to God, Exalted is He. They should neither wrong nor hurt anyone, but should do their utmost to be helpful to their families, their environment, and the society in which they live.

This is why lovers do not say everything that comes to the tip of the tongue, but keep the secrets entrusted to them. They do not investigate and divulge people's faults, and they abstain from backbiting. They strive to ensure that no harm comes to anyone as a result of what they do or say. You cannot pretend to be a lover if you eat whatever comes to hand and say whatever enters your head. Control of sexual desires is also a condition of being a lover. The slave of animal passions cannot be called a lover. One who blindly yields to his every lust, being the slave and client of the flesh, sinks to the state of being the creature and servant not of God, Exalted is He, but of his lower self. He becomes the Devil's plaything, despised and held in contempt by his fellow men. Still, provided he comes to regret this rotten, filthy state, genuinely and sincerely repents and seeks forgiveness, and performs deeds pleasing to God, Exalted is He, he may be rescued from this shameful condition.

God, Glorified and Exalted is He, may pardon and forgive, if He wishes, any sin committed against His Divine Essence, except the sin of ascribing partners to Him. He has definitely stated and clearly explained in his Mighty Koran that He will by no means pardon the setting up of partners in His Essence of Oneness.

We know for certain from the Book and the Hadith that those who repent for any sin, other than that of attributing partners to God, will be as if they had never committed that sin and will be the object of divine pardon. It is also certain that those who turn from polytheism to affirming the Unity of God will achieve the same distinction.

Among God's creatures there are some so dear to Him, Exalted is He, that even if they should sin they would not be held responsible for the sins they have committed, for all they do and say is inspired by the Truth. Those who belong to this group will not be questioned and held to account at the coming Resurrection. The likes of these will not even be brought to the place of final Judgment. They will not see that dreadful terror. While all other creatures are assembled, sweating, to await the Reckoning, these honored beings will be led away to Paradise. These are the lovers of God, Exalted is He. Their sole desire is God and their only purpose is to win the Divine Pleasure. Therefore for them the gates are open to the Paradise of Deeds, the Paradise of Attributes, and the Paradise of Essence. By virtue of the Divine Generosity, these happy and fortunate individuals will enter immediately into the Paradise of the Manifestation of Essence.

It is quite impossible to define love in words or to describe it with the pen. Love is an endless, limitless sea, an unfathomable ocean. Those privileged to receive the blessed gift of love are able to share in it in accordance with their capacity and their lot. Yes, love is infinite, and yet there remains the question of one's capacity and one's lot. Each lover shines with the light he receives, according to his lot and capacity, from this infinite source of light. Everyone receives according to the measure of his cup, and drinks in accordance with his fate, the Divine Love offered by the hand of the All-Powerful. Those who drink it can never come back to their senses, but pass beyond themselves, intoxicated and bewildered. Only through Divine Union can they ever become sober again. It is of course only natural that those who are drunk with love of Him should be able to regain sobriety through union with Him.

O faithful lover!

The greatest miracle is to succeed in bringing back to the true path one who has strayed from that path. It is no miracle to move walls, to waste one's life in pursuit of impossible fantasies, to swallow nails, to hold snakes, to walk upon the water, to appear in various shapes and forms, to fly like a bird, to strike terror on all sides. Perhaps each of these can be considered a clever feat, but such performances are of no benefit to mankind. The only possible justification for such clever tricks is that they may serve to summon shortsighted disbelievers back to the faith.

We know from men of God that many far better than those who walk on water have died of thirst while striving to save mankind from the darkness of ignorance and disbelief.

These happy and fortunate beings do not die—perish the thought—but rather continue to exist. It is only the animal that dies. Those who die for the salvation of mankind do not really die; they remain in being. They rejoice in the realm of eternal love with the True Beloved. Of a certainty, those who lend dignity and honor to history by following their radiant and blessed path will be recorded in annals of gold, and their holy names will be extolled and magnified till the Resurrection.

Those whose hearts and forms are adorned with love of God are always striving to rescue mankind from the degradation of ignorance and unbelief, from the abasement of error. The eyes of such lovers of Truth behold nothing but the Truth. Their ears hear nothing but the words of Truth. Their tongues speak only to remember the Truth and to summon mankind to the Truth. Genuine lovers carry in their hearts nothing but love of the Truth. Thus their feet walk for the sake of the Truth, their hands hold for the sake of the Truth, they work for the sake of the Truth, they speak for the sake of the Truth, they write for the sake of the Truth; because for them nothing exists but the Truth.

Now, to those who lay claim to love I address these questions:

How often have you wiped away the tears of a lover weeping for love of God?

Have you yourself ever shed a single tear for love of God?

How many nights have you spent without sleep for love of God?

What sacrifices have you been able to bear for love of God?

One could add many more such questions, but to what avail? A word to the wise is sufficient. So I remind you once again:

Those who find God within themselves do not search for the Beloved to right or left. Those who seek God outside should know that His irresistible force prevails in worlds upon worlds unknown, from this earth to the Pleiades, and that He is not outside but within the soul, the Soul within the soul. Neither Heaven nor earth contains Him, yet He is at home within the heart of His faithful, sincere, and loving servant. Could it be that those who have experienced the taste of this would not love and remember God? Could it be that those who have achieved such blessedness would not whirl around, calling out "Allah"?

When lover and beloved are found together in one body, what could be more natural than for the lover to whirl in remembrance? Should not the lover perish in that instant, chorusing HAYY . . . HU . . . QAYYUM (Living God . . . He . . . Everlasting)? Churning like the seas, dashing like the waves, should he not call "Allah, Allah . . ." and drown in those vast oceans? Should he not cast himself into the flame like the moth, burn with Divine Love, and have his ashes sown to the wind?

As for people who look askance and cast aspersions on those who whirl in remembrance through Divine Love, can they expect to be able to die in faith? Do they suppose that they will be able to drink the Water of Paradise from the blessed hands of the Beloved Prophet?

Have they no fear of God, Exalted is He, and are they not ashamed before the noble Messenger when slandering the faithful lovers of God—who give their hearts to His beloved Prophet, most excellent greetings to him and his family, who remember God, Exalted is He, and proclaim His Unity, who perform their five daily prayers, who keep the Fast one month a year, who give the obligatory alms, who fulfill the obligation of Pilgrimage, whose eyes are tearful and hearts aflame with the Divine Love, who chorus "Allah, Allah" throughout sleepless nights, who weep to the call of HU as they become annihilated in the Living, Everlasting One? If they themselves cannot remember God and if they cannot join the whirling, what right have they to prevent others from doing so? Does not God, Lord of Majesty and Perfection, say in His Mighty Proof, the Koran:

"Let no set of people deride another, and let women not deride other women who may be better than they are."

Let them try to emulate these lovers of the Truth, let them imitate them, let them attempt to follow in their footsteps. For people are judged with those they imitate. The Leader of the givers of true tidings, the Guide of lovers, the final Prophet has plainly stated that each person shall be resurrected together with the object of his love.

May God, Exalted is He, make us all fellow travelers in our faith, and may He make us intimate companions of the people of love. Amen.

In the glorious Sura of the Noble Koran entitled *al-Ahzab*, God, Glorified and Exalted is He, says:

"Remember Me very, very often."

The frequency of remembrance here commanded indicates that it should be continuous. In conformity with this interpretation, which is based upon authoritative commentaries, others clarify this continuousness as meaning:

"Remember in every state and activity."

It is therefore possible to infer that one may remember God while standing, sitting, or lying down.

This glorious divine decree proves, therefore, that the dhikr is permissible in all conditions, be it while walking in the street or while whirling around. Just as it is permissible to recite the Koran while walking along the road, it is most certainly permissible to remember God in the same circumstances.

Lovers remember God, Glorified and Exalted is He, whatever their condition. During their remembrance their eyes are filled with tears, their hearts are radiant with the love of God, their innermost being is full and vibrant with the fear of God. The eyes of their hearts behold the divine mysteries. They reflect upon their origins and their ultimate destinations. Their hearts are ablaze with the love of God.

While engaged in remembrance, lovers have no desire, wish, or purpose but to seek the good pleasure of God, Exalted is He. Lovers do not practice remembrance for the sake of escaping Hell or entering Paradise. They have no need of Paradise, its pavilions, its handmaidens and servants. As lovers see it, Paradise is "all but" [God]. For lovers burning with love of God, "all but" is certainly not the desired object.

Lovers' prayers are acceptable to God. Lovers do not notice people's faults, for their own failings blind them to those of others. Lovers do not curse nor do they wish harm to anyone at all. Rich and poor are alike to them. The sovereign and the slave are one. No one can comprehend the states of lovers or penetrate their secrets. These states and secrets are known to none save God, Exalted is He, and His lovers. These beautiful virtues are graciously bestowed upon them as a trust from God. Indeed all blessings are from God, Exalted is He. So take care not to look askance at or cast aspersions on the dervishes and lovers. With God is our refuge.

Princess Adile (1825-1898), for whose soul I offer prayers, the daughter of Sultan Mahmud II, known and remembered as Mahmud the Just, has written:

In the way of Truth they *all* forsook—
Cause the dervishes no harm
The Beloved's way was the way they took—
Cause the dervishes no harm.

For dervishes Truth is the way
To neither right nor left they sway
Attain the Truth as saints they may—
Cause the dervishes no harm.

The dervish cannot be described
To meet the Friend they have arrived
Say those to whom perfection is ascribed—
Cause the dervishes no harm.

This worldliness they would decline
To extreme hardship they'd incline
Of Unity they'd drink the wine—
Cause the dervishes no harm.

Adile! Let talking be
The dervish way is calling thee
The face of Truth thyself to see—
Cause the dervishes no harm.

Remembrance of God, Exalted is He, is not confined to any moment, period of time, limits, or place. We may remember Him at any moment, at any time, and in any place without restriction. Indeed, Remembrance of God, Exalted is He, requires no special site. It is permissible to remember Him in any clean place. Nevertheless, while it is permissible to remember God, Exalted is He, in any place, certain sites and locations are undoubtedly preferable to others.

Just as certain Messengers are more highly favored than other Prophets, just as certain men are born to a higher station than other men, so certain sites and locations are definitely of superior merit. We know from the Truthful Informant, may the Creator's blessings be upon him and his family, that Mecca the Ennobled, Medina the Illumined, and the Aqsa Mosque in Jerusalem are of superior merit to other towns and cities. This being known and accepted, we can say quite clearly that the remembrance of God can be performed in any location and in any site that is adequately clean and pure.

It is the duty of man, as God's servant, to correct his lower self through acts of worship and spiritual exercises. For it is only by such means that the lower self can be corrected. By the affirmation of His Unity, God, Glorified and Exalted is He, uproots the lower self which urges and encourages us to wickedness, the self we call *al-nafs al-ammara.* The attainment of complete rectification is conditional upon the lover's observance of constant remembrance, *dhikr da'im.* Moreover the dhikr should not be done absent-mindedly. You must be aware of what you are doing, Whom you are remembering, and what the remembrance is.

People of Truth and reality have handed down this story for our guidance:

When God, Glorified and Exalted is He, had created the self, He asked it: "Who am I?"

The self replied: "You are you. I am I!"

God, Magnified and Glorified is He, then put the self to burn in Hell for a thousand years. Then He took it out and repeated the same question. Receiving the same reply, He put it back to scorch for a further thousand years. Again He took it out, and again the answer was the same. This time God, Lord of Majesty and Perfection, made the self go hungry and thirsty for a thousand years, at the end of which the same question was posed yet again. Meekly the self replied:

"You are the Lord of all the worlds. As for me, I am an impotent, weak, puny, and nevertheless sinful creature."

Upon hearing this answer the Creator made fasting a religious obligation for man.

This parable demonstrates that the improvement of the lower self is possible only through acts of worship and spiritual exercises. It is therefore a necessary prerequisite for lovers that they correct their lower selves by means of worship, spiritual exercises, and Remembrance of God. Through these the self may attain a tranquil character, the heart may be purified, and the spirit burnished.

It must not be forgotten that, on the day of Resurrection, in the hour of remorse and at the moment of regret, you can expect no help from your wealth, your worldly position or rank, your children, or your dependents. Only an Unblemished Heart will profit you then, and the only way by which you can obtain an Unblemished Heart is by remembrance of God.

An Unblemished Heart means a heart that is enlivened by the love of God, enlightened by the love of Muhammad, polished and cleansed by ardent remembrance. Such a heart is called *qalb salim*. The only way to be united with God, Exalted is He, is to possess a heart such as this. Love of God is a flame that burns up and annihilates everything in the heart except the love of God. In such a state, even the most reasonable person may manifest the ecstasy known as *wajd.* When ecstasy like this is induced, one must then and there whirl in worship or else immediately perish, burn up, and be annihilated.

Certain bigots maintain that ecstatic manifestations like whirling are not permissible while one is in his right mind, but can only be performed when he is completely carried away and loses his reason and consciousness. To them the venerable Junayd of Baghdad gave this wise reply:

"To whirl in worship is not unlawful; even if it were unlawful, at this point the unlawful becomes lawful!"

What he is saying is that since certain emergencies render permissible what is normally unlawful, and since a state of emergency exists for the lover in a state of ecstasy, it follows that even if whirling in worship were forbidden by Sacred Law, it must in this case become lawful. To prove his point, the venerable Junayd cites the case where, for a person threatened with starvation, it becomes permissible to eat a sufficient quantity of carrion or pork.

There are two types of intense human enjoyment: (1) the rapture of the physical form and (2) the Reality of rapturous enjoyment. Enjoyment of the physical form is experienced in sexual union with the loved one, and the intense delight tasted in this is called rapture of the physical form. The Reality of rapturous enjoyment is union with the Truth, Exalted is He, and the rapturous joy experienced from this union.

The first of these is satisfied when orgasm is achieved. In the second, if the lover experiences the rapturous Reality and does not express it through whirling in worship, his phantomlike being will naturally be annihilated in the being of the Truth. As his insubstantial being is annihilated, nothing but the Truth will be left in any of his physical organs. All his organs will experience the same blissful joy, will see nothing but the Truth and be aware of nothing but the Truth. Just as someone in a fit of malaria cannot stop trembling, even though still in possession of his mind and will, so is the lover compelled by the force of love to whirl in worship, even though still fully conscious. So much does his love increase as he whirls in worship that to be able to attain such love is clear proof of union with the Lord. This state of exultation is called *wajd khayri,* Beneficent Ecstasy. This Beneficent Ecstasy is, beyond any doubt, one of the greatest blessings and bounties bestowed by God, Exalted is He, upon His servants. This state of rapture is called Beloved of God, Exalted is He, and an Ecstasy of the All-Merciful.

Someone asked our master the most Noble Messenger, may God bless him and give him peace:

"O Messenger of God, how is it that you praise and extol Uways al-Qarani, despite the fact that he does not come to visit you?"

To this God's beloved Prophet gave this felicitous reply:

"Uways cannot come to meet me because in him there is the ecstasy of the All-Merciful."

The noble Uways al-Qarani, may God be pleased with him, did indeed possess such an ecstasy.

This state is a matter not of scholarly learning but of joyful experience. Learning and logic are inadequate when it comes to defining and describing this state. Its joy is known only to those who taste it. Those who have never tasted can never know, nor can it ever be described to them.

When the rememberer begins to remember the Truth, God, Exalted is He, also begins to remember the rememberer. Revealing this secret in the Remembrance itself, He has promised and reminded the heedless that He will honor with His very person the lovers who remember and glorify His Divine Essence. As we have said, a person remembers very often the object of his love. One who remembers God, Exalted is He, does so because of his love for Him. This being so, the Exalted Lord loves his servants who remember Him, grants them His pardon and forgiveness, and offers them Paradise and its splendor. A person is one with the object of his love. In remembrance, rememberer and remembered are surely together as one.

In the glorious Koranic Sura entitled "Repentance" (*al-Tawba*) Almighty God refers to Abraham, on Him be peace, as *awwahun halim*. The meaning of *awwah* is one who often remembers God, Exalted is He, weeping and wailing from fear of God and love of Him. And *halim* means one who forgives those who cause him pain, who responds with good deeds to the bad deeds of others, and who constantly begs his Lord for the ability to forgive those who do him ill.

Through this Koranic verse the Lord of Majesty and Perfection lets us know how it is with His Loyal Friend, instructing us to behave likewise if we seek the friendship of His Divine Essence.

Would the Truth, Glorified and Exalted is He, have heaped such praises upon Abraham, peace be upon him, if audible remembrance were forbidden in the sight of God, Exalted is He, and if it were not considered permissible to cry out ALLAH . . . HU . . . HAYY during sessions of dhikr? Clearly the intention in extolling Abraham, God's Loyal Friend, is to show him as an example for us so that we may always follow his enlightened path.

We have already alluded to those who claim that there is exhibitionism in public dhikr but our answer bears repeating. All we need say is:

"All actions are to be judged according to the intention that precedes them."

Many mysteries come to light in the whirling of the lovers and in their ritual dhikr—for those with eyes to see, of course. As for the blind . . . .

Those who intently observe the movement of the dervishes and lovers as they whirl in worship will come to understand many mysteries and truths. Of course there are many people who attend the rituals of the lovers, and see and hear the dervishes crying LA ILAHA ILLA-LLAH . . . ALLAH . . . HAYY . . . HU, and yet remain totally oblivious of the states experienced by those same dervishes as they remember God, Exalted is He, with love and longing, with endless joy and delight. They do not realize that those lovers and dervishes are inhaling the fragrance of the rose gardens of their Friend and gathering bouquet upon bouquet of eternally fragrant roses from His garden. In the company of their friends they look upon the companions of their Friend. They behold the beauty of the Beloved. They pass from state to indescribable state, from joy to indescribable joy. Only through Remembrance of God is it possible to attain this great blessedness, so if you wish to smell the perfume and to gather the roses of the Friend's garden, to inhale the fragrance of Muhammad, and to be present in this circle of love—stop your denial and come to confirmation! Come blow like the dawn wind in this valley of love. Come walk in the rose gardens of the heart and partake of the joy of the perfume of love so that you may achieve discernment.

Pure let heart and soul be made
Remembrance of the Lord remember
Let love be your stock-in-trade
Remembrance of the Lord remember.

To cross the gate the Sacred Laws obey
This house stands on the Mystic Way
The Truth will give the right to stay
Remembrance of the Lord remember.

Raise the fallen up again
Plunge them in love's ocean main
Help them to achieve their aim
Remembrance of the Lord remember.

With the seekers in their quest
Never pause to take a rest
Let the dervish be your guest
Remembrance of the Lord remember.

If the Sheikh's hand you will take
If your reticence you will forsake
In the Beloved's company you will partake
Remembrance of the Lord remember.

Veliyyuddin, say nothing more
Remembrance cleanse you to the core
Turn now and face the One whom you adore
Remembrance of the Lord remember.

Indeed, neither my attempt to explain nor your effort to understand these truths can be of any avail unless you see how the lovers brand their bodies with the fire of love, how they weep with love and affection for God and His Messenger, how they circle the light of Divine Beauty like moths, how they are filled with radiance while whirling in worship around that light; unless you enter into the lover' s secrets; unless you join the whirling. So come and join the circle: Come and say ALLAH! You have surely heard that those who say ALLAH are not left destitute and sorrowful. Say ALLAH with us, so that you may not be left destitute, so that you may not be in sorrow, so that you do not feel like a stranger.*

God, Glorified and Exalted is He, says in His Mighty Koran:

"Then woe unto those whose hearts are hardened against the remembrance of God" (39:22).

This is interpreted as meaning: Woe unto them, may they suffer the most painful torment, whose hearts harden and contract when they hear the Remembrance of God, Exalted is He, and behold the condition of those who remember Him.

Such are the heedless ones who compare the remembrance of believers to play-acting. Unbelievers and hypocrites only increase in disbelief, hypocrisy, and frustration when they hear the reading of the Noble Koran or the Remembrance of God. Their hearts have become so cramped and narrow that they cannot participate in the remembrance and even turn their backs upon those who perform it. These wretched creatures do not know, it never occurs

*See Appendix.

to them, that those who turn away from the Divine Remembrance are ruined in this world and in the Hereafter, and come to a dreadful end.

Such is the arrogance and envy of some heedless and ignorant people, that they oppose the dhikr of the dervishes. Does it never occur to them that those who turn away from the Divine Remembrance are either unbelievers or hypocrites? Had they so much as one atom of intelligence, they would abandon this arrogance and envy, save themselves from being equated with unbelievers and hypocrites, and rescue their souls from the hell of woe. We are often told in the Noble Hadith, as well as in the Koranic verse quoted above, that those who oppose the Remembrance of God and the affirmation of His Unity, who attack, insult, and injure those who remember God and declare His Unity—these are hypocrites.

On the Day of Resurrection every soul will be summoned to the Divine Presence, along with the record of his achievements in this life. How is it that those who oppose the people of Remembrance fail to realize that they will be summoned in the company of the hypocrites, that they will be filled with remorse, but that this remorse of theirs will not help them in the least? How could any reasonable and sensible person forget that in His glorious Koranic verse "Remember God with much remembrance" (33:41), God, Exalted is He, has ordained that His Divine Essence should be remembered repeatedly and continuously? Even if they themselves cannot obey this glorious divine decree, by what right can they presume to prevent those who faithfully observe it?

One should hold in affection the lovers, Sufis, and dervishes who frequently and constantly remember God, Lord of Majesty and Perfection, for the Prince of the world, God bless Him and give Him peace, said in a noble Hadith:

"A man is together with the one he loves."

Anyone who hopes to be together with those loved by God, Exalted is He, and His faithful lovers, on the Day of Resurrection which is destined and certain to come, should nourish love and affection toward them. It should never be forgotten that affection for those who love God, Exalted is He, is in fact affection for God Himself, Glorified and Exalted is He. It is love of Him. Therefore those who have a little intelligence ought to treat the lovers with affection.

As we constantly reiterate, those who frequently and constantly remember God, Exalted is He, are His beloved. When even we poor helpless mortals look after and protect the ones we love, should not the Lord of Heaven and earth, of all worlds known and unknown, seen and unseen, look after and protect His beloved servants? And should He not love the ones who love His servants? The Supreme Lord gathers those who love the ones He loves together with His loved ones.

O lover!

If you desire the bounty of the declaration of Divine Unity, if you wish to enter the Palace of Oneness, if you long to behold the Everlasting Beauty, then say sincerely LA ILAHA ILLA-LLAH. Affirm the Divine Unity and do so unceasingly. God, Exalted is He, will never leave destitute the one who affirms His Unity. Do not forget that *you* do not exist: *He* exists. If you ascribe existence to yourself, it will become a veil between you and the Truth, Exalted is He, in this world and in the Hereafter. So attribute being to Him alone and rend the intervening veil! He who is obsessed with his own existence, personality, and egoism becomes a devil, becomes like Satan.

When we have before us so many clear Koranic verses and so many Prophetic Hadith expressing approval and encouragement of remembrance and affirmation of the Divine Unity; when so many scholars, Sheikhs, and saints have practiced the Remembrance of God; when lovers by the millions have been known to give value to their fleeting breath in this transient world by remembering and affirming the Divine Unity night and day, morning and evening, always and everywhere; those heedless people who molest the rememberers, who injure and offend them in word or deed, will realize their great mistake when the Resurrection comes. In great remorse they will tear out their hair and beards, but this last-minute regret will benefit them not at all.

The same punishment will be meted out to the ignorant fools who are so taken in by the words of the envious that they presume to criticize and even despise the people of Remembrance. To stand clear of the likes of these is to be close to God, Exalted is He. What can one do but pray for the guidance of the heedless, the ignorant, and their pitiful followers, who are supposedly well read but do not understand anything of what they read?

How can the joy and delight of the remembrance and affirmation of Divine Unity be experienced by those unfortunates who have not drunk the Wine of Oneness from the Hand of Power, who have not abandoned themselves heart and soul in the way of love, who cannot distinguish black and white and are therefore inevitably unaware of the Divine Love and have no guide on the way of life? The aggressive assaults of this mob actually rebound upon themselves. Only if it is for the sake of God may certain criticisms sometimes be justified. But criticisms at variance with the divine decree and Prophetic command, since they stem from the temptation of the lower self and the Devil, will certainly be requited by God, Exalted is He, in accordance with their intention. As we are among those who always recommend the Truth, however, we give them this advice:

Such enviers and disbelievers should repent and seek God's forgiveness before death overtakes them. Nor should they be satisfied with repentance and seeking forgiveness alone; they must abandon their ugly qualities. The only way for them to achieve this is by finding a wise and godly spiritual guide, holding the hand of this blessed and noble being, submitting to him completely, and learning the truth and reality from this knower of the wisdom of God.

May God, Lord of Majesty and Perfection, pardon and forgive us all and remember our names among His happy and beloved servants.

"Pride bars the way to happiness," they say.

To escape their bad condition, therefore, those who are trapped in arrogant pride must rid their minds of all they have ever learned, pour away the stagnant water from their pitchers, cleanse the mirror of their hearts of all envy, spite, hatred, and hypocrisy, wipe away all false pretense, seek ways and means of learning esoteric knowledge, be enlightened by the light of Divine Unity, become conscious through whirling in worship, rejoice in the love of God, seek the mysteries of divine wisdom, and be eager to remember and affirm the Unity of God. It will then be quite possible for them to color themselves with *sibghatullah* (God's dye) and to awaken from the sleep of unconsciousness. Each of them may then become a sincere and perfect believer, and they may be admitted into the mysteries of the lovers. They may win the right to see the One they seek, and to achieve the good pleasure of the Beloved.

O lover!

According to the tradition of the saints, ecstasy—*wajd**—is a light in the heart of the believer which urges and encourages him to worship God, Glorified and Exalted is He. Indeed, our master the Messenger of God, God bless him and give him peace, said:

"He who has no *wajd* has no faith."

We have reminded the reader on various occasions that "all acts are valued according to intentions." When beginning Remembrance of God, it is therefore necessary to say first of all: "I intend to find ecstasy."

If someone pronounces the Testimony (that there is none worthy of worship but God and that Muhammad is His Messenger), if he sincerely believes this profession of faith and approaches the worship of God, Exalted is He, with his heart polished by this testimony, that person is one of the ecstatics, the people of *wajd*. For this condition can only be gained and acquired through affection and

*The root of this Arabic word is *wajada,* meaning "to find." One who finds God, Exalted is He, within himself through the love and fear of God in his heart, possesses *wajd*.

longing for Almighty God, and this is in proportion with one's intention.

In order to perform whirling there must be a conscious intention to find ecstasy. The whirling in worship performed by the lovers is sanctioned by the Consensus of the Community. The whirling rituals, which constitute the fundamental practices of the saints of God, were formulated in the time of the Successors to the Companions of the Prophet, and their judgment was subsequently confirmed and corroborated by the scholars of the next generation and the noble founders of the science of Islamic jurisprudence. Consequently, not one of the revered personalities who came and went between the years 80 and 800 of the Hijra ever said that whirling in worship is unlawful. Only after the year A.H. 800 have there appeared certain shortsighted, narrow-minded fanatics, self-styled scholars who have put forward the view that whirling in worship is unlawful and have tried to ban it.

However, very many of the great scholars and perfected saints did participate in ritual remembrance and whirling. The vast majority of the Koranic commentators, collectors of Hadith, compilers, authors, scholars, and initiates used to practice remembrance and whirling. These were all men celebrated not only in their own lifetime, but long after their passing, for their learning and charismatic powers, men of vision and spiritual insight so many of whom joined an order of Truth-seekers. The saints whose lives and work have been written about and others whose stories have not been written down would fill countless tomes, and all of them whirled in worship for the love of God. May God, Glorified and Exalted is He, sanctify their souls.

One of these revered beings is al-Sheikh al-Akbar (the Greatest Sheikh), Muhyiddin ibn al-'Arabi. According to a work entitled *al-Janib al-Gharbi* (The Western Region), the venerable Sheikh was the author of nearly a thousand books. One of the most important of his works is undoubtedly his commentary on the Koran, a painstaking and highly esteemed interpretation called *al-Jam' wa-l-Tafsil fi Asrar al-Tanzil.* Its sixty-four volumes carry us to the noble verse in the glorious Sura *al-Kahf*: *wa-idh qala musa li-fatahu la abrahu* "And when Moses said to his servant: I will not give up . . ." (18:60), which means that this commentary covers only half of the Mighty Koran. His *al-Futuhat al-Makkiya* (Meccan Revelations) consists of twenty-four volumes. Of his other works some are shorter and some are longer than this. The two-volume commentary attributed to the venerable Sheikh is not by him but by Kashani.

My venerable master, my benefactor and revered teacher, told me that he once had the privilege of seeing a document written in the hand of the venerable Sheikh authorizing his stepson, Sadruddin of Konya, to transmit his teaching. In this document he read the titles of 267 works by him.

The venerable Sadruddin of Konya relates that the Greatest Sheikh once went for nine months without food, drink, or sleep. Throughout this period he continuously proclaimed the Unity of the Truth, Exalted is He, and never ceased for one instant from the Remembrance of God. May God, Glorified and Exalted is He, sanctify his spirit.

The venerable Sheikh Abu Ishaq al-Firuzabadi, author of the famous Arabic dictionary, relates the following story in his biography of the Greatest Sheikh, entitled *al-I'tiyad:*

When the venerable Sheikh Muhyiddin ibn al-'Arabi, may the Creator sanctify his Spirit, had finished writing his monumental work *al-Futuhat al-Makkiya,* he left the manuscript in an exposed place on the walls of the revered Kaaba with this prayer: "My Lord! If this work of mine should meet with Your noble approval, preserve it from all calamities!" That year in Mecca the Ennobled, the rain, wind, and storms were beyond description, and yet, strange to relate, no harm befell one leaf, not even a single letter of the manuscript left uncovered on the wall. It was neither spoiled nor scattered nor torn.

Since so many noble Sheikhs and pious scholars, well versed in esoteric knowledge and famous for their learning and charismatic powers, have not only considered the Remembrance of God and whirling in worship to be permissible but have advanced clear and decisive evidence to this effect, no value or significance can be attached to opposition on the part of people incapable even of reading and understanding works written by these blessed and fortunate individuals, or to their impudent attempts to have them declared unlawful.

Everything in heaven and earth and in between glorifies God, Exalted is He. This is why God, Glorified and Exalted is He, says in His Noble Koran:

"There is nothing that does not glorify, extol, and remember Me. But you cannot understand their praise and remembrance."

If those who maintain that whirling in worship is unlawful, and who would presume to have it banned, should object that they cannot see things glorifying God and whirling in worship and cannot hear their remembrance, we shall again answer those disbelievers by quoting the words of God:

"To you the mountains appear solid and stationary. But the mountains are not solid and stationary as they appear to you. Just as clouds traverse the sky, so do the mountains become transported until they are seen no more. Is not this truth plain to heedless ones like you?"

If we plunge a straight stick into still water, the stick appears crooked, whereas in reality it is absolutely straight. The defect is in our own vision. How many things appear similarly distorted or wrong although they are really correct, the distortion lying again only in our own vision and perception.

Everything that has an existence revolves within its own being. Nothing in this world or the Hereafter is standing still. This truth, familiar to the experts, has been proved and documented by the positive sciences. Sun, moon, stars, and all that exists revolve with the love of God. The entire Universe is dancing and whirling with God's love.

With hidden wisdom in the being of Truth you know us.
In the endless ocean of secret knowledge you know us.
The nightingales of this temporal rose garden will not hear us.
Lovers of the beauty of His Eternal Face will know us.
We care not to rebuild this world or the Next.
Those who stumble and are ruined will know us.
We left our senses, dropped the cloak from our shoulders.
Strip yourself bare, be naked to know us.
They suffer who do not know that pain and joy are one.
The sultan saved from torment knows us.
The hermit who stays sober will not understand us.
One drunk on the last gulp of the wine of purity will know us.
It is for man to heed the wise one's every word.
Do not suppose that those who live like animals will know us.
O Niyazi! We are but a drop that fell in the ocean today.
What knowledge can a drop possess?
Only the ocean knows us.

7

THE WORLD OF WITNESSING AND THE WORLD OF RESURRECTION

O lover of God!

Dance and whirl with the Divine Love! Chant ALLAH . . . HAYY, the Ever-Living . . . HU, all is contained in Him . . . QAYYUM, the Self-Existent. The sea of Unity boiled with love of the Essence of Oneness and the Universe of Souls became manifest in the Universe of Divine Power. In its motion it began to remember and glorify God, Exalted is He. Thus it descended to the Angelic Universe. Then the worlds were created. The Universe of Dominion descended glorifying and extolling, then the visible world appeared. That is why this world we live in is called the World of Witnessing (the material universe). From this world, and then from the intermediate realm called *Barzakh,* we pass on to the world of Judgment and Resurrection, to the final station and abode which is either Paradise or Hell. And none of these levels we have enumerated is ever stationary; they are in constant motion.

All creation animate or inanimate, all matter that we consider lifeless, is in constant motion. Only the Void is motionless. All created things remember and glorify God, Exalted is He, in accordance with their proper motions. In His noble Sura *Ya-Sin*, God, Glorified and Exalted is He, informs us that the sun, the moon, and all the stars remember and glorify His Most Glorious and Exalted Essence in the rotation of their orbits. This Sea of Unity belonging to the Divine Essence is called in Sufi terminology the Inconceivable Universe.

One day, a desert Arab who enjoyed the happy privilege of paying his humble respects in the radiant presence of the Glorious Messenger, asked: "O Messenger of God, before these Universes were created, where was our Lord God, great is His Glory?"

The Beloved of God replied: "He was in the Inconceivable Universe."

We cannot ask about the location of this Universe, for the Inconceivable Universe has neither name nor place nor definition. Human reason and intellect are incapable of forming any conception of this Universe. This Universe defies every hypothesis, delimitation, and qualification. It is utterly impossible for human beings to know and understand this Universe. Only God, Lord of Majesty and Perfection, can know this Universe with the knowledge of His Essence of Oneness.

According to the Sacred Tradition "I was a hidden treasure. I wished to make this treasure known, so I created creation," the Sea of Oneness is a Universe unmanifest and unknown to man, angels, and other creatures. It became manifest through the vibration of His Essence, and the Universe of Souls made its appearance. The starting point of the emerging Universe of Souls is the Light of Muhammad, God bless him and give him peace. This is why the First Principle of the Universe, God bless him and give him peace, said:

"God, Honored and Glorified is He, first of all created my Light. Together with my Light and my Spirit, the Pen was created. Mine was also the first self to be created. When Adam, peace be upon him, was between earth and water, I was already a Prophet."

The meaning we can deduce from this terse statement is that it refers in reality to the Universe of Souls. This Universe is also called the Universe of Oneness, as well as the Universe of Plurality, the First Determination, the Universe of Confirmation, and the Universe of Testing. The name Universe of Souls is given to that Universe in which Almighty God addressed the souls with the question "Am I not your Lord?" and received the reply "Yes, You are our Lord! We acknowledge you and bear witness thereto." In other words this acknowledgment and testimony occur in the Universe of Souls. This acknowledgment, glorification, and attestation are never absent for a single instant from the Universe of Souls.

The souls are then brought down from the Universe of Souls to the Angelic Universe, and from there down to the Universe of Dominion, the material world in which we live. The next step is to the world called *Barzakh*, the intermediate world which is also known as the World of the Tomb. From here the souls are brought to another world called the World of Eternity. This is the last world, the completion of the journey. The people of Paradise will reach Paradise, while the people of Hell will enter Hell, and there in their respective abodes they will stay forever. In each of these various worlds the creatures of God, Exalted is He, will not be able to cease glorifying and remembering Him for one moment, as the Exalted Lord has explained in the noble verse of His Mighty Proof, the Koran: "There is not one creature that does not remember Me, that does not praise Me. Yet you do not hear or understand their remembrance and praise."

This judgment applies to all except Prophets and saints of God, for God, Exalted is He, has enabled these honored few to hear all things remembering and glorifying Him. These highly favored and extraordinary beings are known as Those Endowed with Perception. They are the only exceptions to the rule.

The venerable Imam 'Ali, may God ennoble his countenance and be pleased with him, said:

"Once when traveling with God's Messenger, God bless him and give him peace, to one of the villages of Medina the Illumined, I heard things along the road greeting the Beloved of God, and then continually remembering God, Exalted is He."

In His Mighty Proof, the Koran, God, Glorified and Exalted is He, informed the Prince of the two worlds of all His judgments and decrees in the form of commands and prohibitions. This being so, why did God, Lord of Majesty and Perfection, Who is All-Knowing and All-Wise and Who knows the true state and condition of His beloved Prophet and his Community, why did He never—neither in the Wise Koran nor in the Prophetic Hadith—forbid Remembrance and whirling in worship? Out of the thousands of commands and prohibitions of God, Exalted is He, in the Noble Koran, can you point to one by which Remembrance and whirling in worship is forbidden? On the contrary, the Koran, in Sura *al-Zumar* (39:75), proves that the angels circle the Throne of God, Exalted is He, whirling around it unceasingly.

Furthermore, our Prophet, the pride of the Universe, God bless him and give him peace, saw in the course of his Ascension that the angels were circling the Prosperous House and reported that they whirl around it.

As for our brother Pilgrims, when they are performing the prescribed ritual Pilgrimage, do they not circumambulate the revered Kaaba?

Can all this evidence possibly fail to satisfy those who stupidly deny the Remembrance of God and the whirling in worship which is one of the fundamental practices of the saints?

Knowledge is knowledge to know;
Knowledge is yourself to know;
Since yourself you do not know,
What's the use of reading so?

Knowledge is the point in reading,
Thus the Truth to come to know;
Since your reading teaches nothing,
That's a fruitless way to go.

"I know from reading"—don't say so!
"I'm so pious"—don't say so!
If the Truth you do not know,
What a useless way to go.

Syllables you read aplenty,
You have spelled out eight and twenty;
With that alphabet go gently,
What's the meaning of it all?

Yunus Emre says: "O sages,
Far better are the wages,
Than for a hundred pilgrimages,
Of entering a human heart."

Rulings on Worship

In matters of religious doctrine the Imams of the Sufi fraternity are the Imams of the Sunna and the Community, Sheikh Abu Mansur al-Maturidi and Sheikh Abu Hasan al-Ash'ari.

In matters of religious practice their Imams are the Greatest Imam Abu Hanifa, Imam al-Shafi'i, Imam Ahmad ibn Hanbal, and Imam Malik. May God have mercy on them all. All Sufis follow one or other of these four revered Imams, among whose teachings there are certain differences in detail only. They all follow the way of the People of the Sunna and the Community and belong to *al-Firqa al-Najiya*, the only group destined for salvation out of the seventy-three religious groupings. Their dogma, doctrine, and belief are all in accordance with the wishes of God's Messenger, God bless him and give him peace, and coincide with the teachings of his Companions and their Successors of the next two generations, as well as all the righteous early believers.

The beliefs and doctrines of these revered individuals never suffered any admixture of heretical innovation or capriciousness. They all observed the wish and intention of the Noble Prophet, following in the blessed and enlightened footsteps of his Companions, their Successors, and all the righteous early believers. That is why those who follow them are known as People of the Sunna and the Community. Like all who tread the elevated Path, dervishes and lovers share the beliefs of the People of the Sunna and the Community and therefore follow one or other of these four Imams.

This being so, the Sufi and dervish fraternity cannot be heretical innovators and capricious eccentrics. Those who stupidly attach such labels to the lovers are obviously ignorant and heedless people who are ill-informed even as to the doctrines of the schools they themselves belong to.

Heretical innovators and capricious eccentrics are those who cannot clean their backbiting tongues of worthless, meaningless, and empty words; who cannot empty their hearts of lies, slander, and calumny; who say whatever comes into their heads without thinking whether it is right or wrong; who fill the houses of their hearts with spite, envy, hatred, and arrogance; whose bad and ugly character continually offends all around them; from whose hands and tongues no one is safe. Truth to tell, it is these slaves of their lower selves, servants of the Devil and captives of their desires, who are the real heretics.

None of these bad qualities can exist in a man who possesses one atom of Divine Love, because his heart is enlightened by the affirmation of Divine Unity and rejoices in that Divine Love. In fact, the Remembrance of God purifies the heart of such bad and ugly qualities. As fire restores the luster of rusted iron, so does the fire of God's love remove the dirt and stains from the hearts of those who remember Him and it saves those who so remember. They are liberated from the trouble and sorrow of both worlds. Yes, the polish for the mirror of the heart is the affirmation of Divine Unity. The tongues and hearts of those who make this affirmation are certainly rendered pure and shining. As the Sultan of the Prophets, most perfect greetings to him and his family, says:

"All things have a polish. The polish of the heart is the Remembrance of God."

Whirling in worship is one of the fundamental practices of the Sufi orders. The first to perform it was the most Noble Messenger, God bless him and give him peace. When Gabriel the Trustworthy brought the divine decree to God's beloved Prophet with the good tidings: "O messenger of God, the poor of your community will enter Paradise five hundred years before the rich communities," the Prince of the two worlds, the noble Ahmad Mahmud Muhammad, on him be peace, went into ecstasy and spun around so much that the cloak fell from his blessed shoulders to the ground. On witnessing this, the noble Companions, may God be pleased with them all, also began to whirl together with the Master of the Sacred Law, most excellent salutations to him and his family.

Seeing the Glory of the Universe, God bless him and give him peace, whirling with his companions, Mu'awiya ibn Abu Sufyan said: "O Messenger of God, what a beautiful dance that is." But our great Master vouchsafed this felicitous reply: "Silence, O Mu'awiya! This is no dance; it is Remembrance of the Beloved. When one hears the Name of one's Beloved is it not good to whirl in worship?" This incident is reported in *'Awarif ul-Ma'arif* on the authority of Anas ibn Malik, may God be pleased with him.

The second person to whirl in worship was our noble master Abu Bakr the Veracious, may God be pleased with him. For the sake of God he had disposed of all his wealth, property, and possessions, so that he had only one shirt left. He and his revered wife used to wear this shirt by turns. Thus they were able to perform their acts of worship to God, Exalted is He, one at a time. One day, God's beloved Prophet said to his loyal Companions: "It is now some days since I saw Abu Bakr in the mosque."

The Companions, may God be pleased with them all, answered: "O Prophet of God, since Abu Bakr has distributed all his property he has not a single thing to wear. That is why he cannot come to the mosque."

The Prince of the two worlds said to them: "Go to my daughter Fatima and ask her for something for Abu Bakr to wear."

When our mother, the lovely lady Fatima, received the Prophet's command, she said that she had nothing but a piece of cloth woven from goat's hair, so at the Prophet's bidding this cloth was sent to Abu Bakr the Veracious. However, since this piece of cloth was not big enough to cover the blessed body of the Most Veracious, he covered the parts left bare with date leaves before leaving his house to enter the radiant presence of the Messenger. At that moment Gabriel, on him be peace, descended wearing an ill-fitting cloth woven of goat's hair, with date leaves to cover the parts left bare. When God's beloved saw this state of affairs he exclaimed in amazement: "My brother Gabriel, I have never seen you dressed like this before."

Gabriel replied: "O Messenger of God, because Abu Bakr is dressed like this, God has today ordered all His creatures in Heaven to wear the same attire. God, Honored and Glorified is He, greets Abu Bakr with peace and asks: 'I am pleased with My servant Abu Bakr. Is My servant Abu Bakr also pleased with Me?"

It was at this moment that the Most Veracious entered the Prophet's mosque, and on hearing this good news from the very mouth of the blessed Messenger, he cried: "I am pleased, I am pleased," and with tears in his eyes he began to whirl.*

One day the Glory of the Universe, God bless him and give him peace, said to the Valiant Lion Imam 'Ali, may God ennoble his countenance and be pleased with him: "O 'Ali, you are of me." The King of Sainthood thereupon began to whirl.

*From Imam al-Ghazali's work entitled *Ihya 'Ulumiddin,* in the section *Kitab al-Tawhid wa-l-Sama'.*

On another occasion the noble Messenger, on him and his family be the blessings of God the All-Bountiful, said to the venerable Ja'far, may God be pleased with him: "Of all men you have the character most closely resembling mine." The venerable Ja'far ibn Abi Talib began to whirl as soon as he heard these words.*

Dancing may not be explicitly permitted in the Sacred Law, but neither is it positively unlawful. Perhaps it comes into the category of legally indifferent natural acts like sitting down and standing up. Therefore, since well-intentioned whirling is permissible, it can undoubtedly be an act of worship when so intended, because in whirling we are remembering God, Exalted is He, and Divine Remembrance is lawful always and everywhere and with whatever movements it may be expressed. Those who remember God, Exalted is He, will certainly receive recompense and reward from their Lord.

While all prescribed acts of worship performed for Almighty God have a definite beginning and ending and a set pattern, the Remembrance of God or Divine Remembrance is not structured in the same way. This is because God, Glorified and Exalted is He, has ordered and commanded us to remember His Divine Essence very, very often. Those whose hearts find tranquility and calm, who experience joy and delight in Remembrance of their Lord and in whirling in worship, and who hope in this way to reach the object of their striving and attain God's Mercy, will most certainly not be left destitute by God, Glorified and Exalted is He, Who will shower His blessings and bounty upon His servants and bring them to salvation and success.

The following story is related by the Greatest Sheikh, Ibn 'Arabi, in *al-Futuhat al-Makkiya*. It deserves to be read with the utmost care and attention:

Sheikh Ja'far ibn Muhammad al-Khalwati and the venerable Junayd al-Baghdadi were traveling to the Hijaz with the intention of performing the Pilgrimage. On their way they visited the Holy City

*In chapter 22 of *'Awarif al-Ma'arif*, Sheikh Shihabuddin al-Suhrawardi says: "Some lunatics dance when the state of ecstasy occurs."

of Jerusalem and Mount Sinai. They reached the place where the Prophet Moses, on him be peace, held a thousand and one conversations with the Lord of the Universe. Standing where Moses, on him be peace, had stood, they offered prayers and supplications. Ecstatic with the grandeur and sanctity of this lofty place, the venerable Junayd al-Baghdadi requested one of his disciples who possessed a beautiful voice to recite a eulogy. While he was chanting, the venerable Sheikh and his dervishes were overcome with love and longing and began to whirl in ecstasy. At this point a Christian monk, who happened to be nearby, witnessed the scene and cried out in amazement to the caravan of lovers: "O people of Muhammad!" But the dervishes in their ecstasy did not hear the monk's call. He cried out again three times, but still no one answered him, as they had all left themselves in their ecstasy as if transported to another world. By the time the monk came right up to them, the dervishes had finished whirling and emerged from their ecstatic state. Approaching the assembled lovers, he then asked: "Which of you is your master?"

The venerable Junayd al-Baghdadi replied: "There are no differences among us. We are all chiefs and masters."

The monk insisted, saying: "Surely there must be a chief among you. Who is he that I may speak to him?"

The dervishes then pointed to the venerable Junayd, and the following conversation ensued:

"Is this ecstatic whirling of yours characteristic of Muslims in general, or is it exclusive to a particular group?" asked the monk.

"The lovers are the only group within the Community of Muhammad who perform this kind of whirling," replied Junayd.

"With what intention do you perform this whirling ritual?" asked the monk.

"Our sole intention is to express our love of God, Glorified and Exalted is He, and the blissful joy we experience in remembering Him," replied Junayd.

"For what reason do you call out aloud the Glorious Name of God, Exalted is He, in the course of your whirling?" asked the monk.

"We do this with the intention of offering ourselves in service to Almighty God," replied Junayd.

"When the Truth, Exalted is He, asked all the souls in the Universe of Souls: 'Am I not your Lord?' the souls replied: 'Indeed, we so testify.' What is this called?" asked the monk.

"This is called the Eternal Proclamation," replied Junayd.

"You have spoken truly, O Sheikh! Come, stretch out to me those blessed hands." Then the monk held the hand of the venerable Sheikh, bore witness to his belief that there is none worthy of worship but Allah and that Muhammad is His Messenger, and was honored with true faith.

The venerable Junayd al-Baghdadi asked the monk: "How did you know that I had spoken the truth?"

The old monk answered with all the sincerity of a new believer: "I know from the noble Gospel that the lovers of the Community of Muhammad wear the dervish cloak, eat crumbs of bread, are content and satisfied with little, love God, Exalted is He, and experience great joy and happiness in remembering Him. They are the lovers of God, Glorified and Exalted is He. They go into ecstasy with love of God and seek to follow His way. They fear God, Exalted is He, and seek His good pleasure in all that they do. I perceived all these qualities in you and your dervishes and—all praise belongs to God!—I have been honored with admission to Islam."

This most holy person joined that caravan of lovers for three days; then on the third day he passed into Eternity as a Muslim and entered Paradise.

God, Magnified and Glorified is He, has mentioned the lovers of the Community of Muhammad both in the noble Gospel and in the other heavenly Books and has praised them most highly. A noble Koranic verse in the glorious Sura entitled *al-Fat'h* confirms the truth of this statement.

Ja'far ibn Abi Talib, may God be pleased with him, one of the noble Companions and a cousin of the glorious Messenger, had been obliged to migrate to Abyssinia. We have it on the authority of Abu Zubayr and Jabir, may God be pleased with them both, that he danced for joy when he was eventually able to return from exile and meet again with the beloved Prophet, and that he was still dancing when he kissed the Prince of the Two Worlds on his blessed forehead.

At the time of the revelation of the noble Koranic verse: "Then when Zayd had duly divorced her . . . ," God's beloved Prophet recited this glorious divine decree to Zayd ibn Harith, may God be pleased with him. Zayd asked: "O Messenger of God, has this noble verse been revealed concerning me?"

The Glory of Creation, most excellent salutations to him and his family, vouchsafed this reply: "Yes, O Zayd, it has been revealed about you and mentions your name." When he heard this, Zayd ibn Harith started dancing.

What more need be said? It must by now be quite clear to any intelligent reader that whirling in worship must be permissible and in accordance with the Sacred Law, since it was practiced by God's beloved Prophet, by Abu Bakr the Most Veracious, by 'Ali the Chosen, by Ja'far ibn Abi Talib, and by Zayd ibn Harith, may God be pleased with them all. Moreover, we know from reliable tradition that the Mother of the Believers, Aisha the Faithful, may God be pleased with her and with her father, watched in the company of the most noble Messenger as the Abyssinians performed their dances.

As we have explained above, the permissibility of dancing is definitely established according to Imam al-Shafi'i, Imam Malik, Imam Ahmad ibn Hanbal, and the Proof of Islam, Imam al-Ghazali, as well as other prominent Sheikhs and scholars. It has even been said that, if done with the right intention, it may sometimes be an act of worship.

The Mystery of Whirling

The Khalwati (in Turkish, Halveti) Order is one of the branches of the Elevated Way that remember God, Exalted is He, audibly or overtly. The members of this order remember Almighty God by performing turning or circling movements. On the basis of its symbolism and inner meaning, the ritual of whirling in Remembrance of God has been judged acceptable by revered individuals renowned for their saintliness, uniquely qualified in Divine Wisdom, preeminent in Divine Love, and celebrated for their esoteric knowledge. The first to pronounce a legal opinion on the Sufi practice of whirling was the Qadi Wahiduddin, sanctified be his spirit. This pronouncement dates from the generation of the Successors and—all praise belongs to God—remains in force to this very day.

Of the founders of the four schools of Islamic law, the Imams al-Shafi'i, Malik, and Ahmad ibn Hanbal all consider whirling to be lawful. Only the Lamp of the Community, the Greatest Imam Abu Hanifa, has nothing to say on this subject, neither forbidding it as unlawful nor pronouncing it specifically permissible. However, his two disciples Imam Yusuf and Imam Muhammad, both of them jurists of the first rank, issued pronouncements to the effect that whirling was lawful. Consequently, the opinion of the two Imams concerning whirling in worship is the one in force in the Hanafi school. The definitive proof of the legality of the whirling prompted by Divine Love is the noble Koranic verse 75 of the glorious Sura *al-Zumar*, which is interpreted as meaning: "You will see the angels encircling the Throne, praising and glorifying their Lord."

It is clearly to be understood from this noble Koranic verse that the angels revolve around the Exalted Throne as they glorify their Lord. Just as the ritual prayers we Muslims perform (whether obligatory, optional, or supererogatory) are modeled on the acts of worship of the angels, so does the noble whirling ritual evolved by the Sufis reflect the worship of the angels of the Exalted Throne, for it is seen as a circling* just like theirs in Remembrance of the Truth.†

Just as the Pilgrims chant supplications and exclaim ALLAHU AKBAR while performing their circumambulation of the revered Kaaba, just as the angels revolve around their gatherings for learning and remembrance, so do the lovers and dervishes who follow the way of the Halveti Order make circling movements while reciting aloud the Divine Names HAYY, ALLAH, QAYYUM, DA'IM, AHAD, SAMAD (Ever-Living, Allah, Self-Existent, Everlasting, One, Eternal). Just as worldly people make the rounds from door to door in search of worldly benefits, so do the lovers of God, Exalted is He, go around calling the Divine Name for the sake of the good pleasure of the Creator, and thus they attain the station which is their goal.

A desert Arab who enjoyed the privilege of entering the radiant presence of the glorious Messenger asked:

"O Messenger of God, does whirling and circling take place in Paradise on high?"

God's Messenger, God bless him and give him peace, remained silent and gave no reply. Just then Gabriel, on him be peace, descended and by divine decree informed the Prince of the two worlds that whirling and circling would be performed in Paradise on high every Friday, the day of Congregation.

O faithful lover! In Paradise there is neither ritual prayer nor fasting, yet there is whirling and turning as an expression of the love of God. Good tidings for the lovers!‡

*The word generally translated as "whirling"—*dawran* in Arabic, *devran* in Turkish—is derived from the same Arabic root as the word for "circle."
†See Appendix.
‡See Appendix.

Human Reason and Divine Mystery

One of the supreme gifts with which God, Glorified and Exalted is He, has blessed and endowed mankind is reason. Where there is reason there is modesty, and where there is modesty there is faith.

This should not be taken to mean that reason can weigh and measure everything. No intellect is capable of grasping the essence and reality of the Creator, for the scales of reason cannot weigh that power.

The mind always seeks its own advantage. It stays out of places where there is no profit to be had.

Human reason is of two kinds: that which enjoys divine guidance and that which lacks it.

Those whose minds are without divine guidance will sink to any depths in pursuit of their own advantage. Consider the following example:

A gang of thieves use their intellect devoid of divine guidance to plan a robbery. They may often succeed through getting these plans exactly right. Even if they should be arrested, those same minds devoid of divine guidance may be able to find ways and means for them to escape and save their skins. All this is possible and can happen, yet I ask you in all conscience: Could you call such people intelligent?

The only treasure in the world worth envying is reason. Look how fond everyone is of his own reason, how he boasts of it and thinks there is nothing it cannot overcome. Yet examine the actions and conduct of such a person and all you see is a set of behavior patterns bearing no relation to reason.

The mind directed by divine guidance, on the other hand, always leads a man to what is good, true, and beautiful. This is the treasure of reason described as *wadi'atullah,* a divine endowment. The commands and prohibitions of God, Exalted is He, can be inculcated in those who possess this treasure. This mind possesses the capacity for distinguishing right from wrong, good from bad, and beautiful from ugly. It can separate and distinguish the true from the false. However, there are still certain divine secrets that can never be perceived or grasped even by this intellect.

During the Prophet's Heavenly Journey, Gabriel, on him be peace, accompanied him as far as the Ultimate Lotus Tree, but there he stopped, saying: "O Messenger of God, this is the farthest limit for me. If I take one more step I shall burst into flames." This is a sign that reason can reach only as far as that Tree and can go no further. In other words, the mind has its limit too, and no one can cross that boundary.

Beyond the mind lies a whole range of universes, inexpressible and inexplicable through human reason, logic, or intellect. Those worlds and their mysteries cannot be weighed in the scales of reason and logic. Anyone attempting to measure by such means will have the balance of his mind broken and his logic thrown into utter confusion.

What is accessible to the mind is almost nothing compared with the many secrets that cannot be reached and measured by the intellect or unraveled by logic. Of course everyone needs reason and intellect, but there are limits to what can be achieved with these instruments.

As we have said, reason and logic always pursue their own interests. They look no further than this. Besides, they sometimes make mistakes. What one sees as reasonable and logical may very often prove harmful.

The divine mysteries and love lie far beyond reason and logic. Let it not be thought that we are rejecting and negating reason and logic. It is just that we are trying to emphasize that many things cannot be understood by these means and that for them many riddles must remain insoluble.

As we know, it was the Devil who first invented logic. The Devil it was who defended himself with his own shortsighted logic against God, Exalted is He. When God, Magnified and Glorified is He, put to him the question: "Why did you not prostrate yourself before Adam?" the Devil replied: "O Lord, You have created me from fire, whereas you have created Adam from earth. And fire is superior to earth." Thus he introduced the principle of logical analogy, and was certainly wrong and mistaken. Since it is quite impossible to unravel the divine mysteries with the mind or by analogical reasoning, his objection on this basis brought about his banishment from the Divine Mercy.

The clear moral of this tale is that we cannot measure everything by reason and logic, and that those who copy the Devil's vain attempt to do so will end up equally bankrupt and satanic.

Once a man was passing a mental hospital. He called out to one of the patients peering through the windows: "How many madmen are there in this hospital?"

Looking the questioner up and down, the inmate replied: "Why don't you leave us alone? There are statistics on us. But tell me, how many sane people are there out there?"

Indeed, the earth's surface is covered with madmen who suppose themselves sane, while beneath it the earth is full of corpses. This fact we should always remember. You honest seekers after the Truth, who desire God's pleasure and love the eternal Beauty, I offer you a prescription which you should always keep in mind: Know! Find! Be!

If you seek the enlightened way leading to the pleasure of God, Exalted is He, if you desire to know your Lord, the precondition is to know yourself. For he who knows himself also knows his Lord. As for God, Exalted is He, only through God can He be known. He who does not know cannot find, and he who does not find cannot be. He remains undeveloped.

There are as many ways to Almighty God as there are breaths in all created beings; this fact is well known and accepted. However, the shortest way is the way indicated and pointed out by God's beloved Prophet, most perfect salutations to him and his family.

This way can easily be traversed by following him and treading in his enlightened and blessed footsteps.

If we look at things in their true light, we will see that even a microbe can lead man to the Truth. The correctness of this observation will be apparent to those who see in everything the manifestation of the Divine and the power of the All-Glorious. But it all depends on the one who sees and hears. The manifestation of the Divine is as clear as day in every single atom, and whichever way one turns the Power of the All-Glorious is apparent. Every atom in the whole universe is acknowledging, glorifying, and extolling Almighty God. Yet this great blessing is denied to those who see only with their ordinary eyes and not with the eye of the heart, who hear with the ears on the sides of their heads, but not with the ear of the heart.

The Sacred Law and The Seeker of the Truth

As we have said, the shortest way leading to God, Glorified and Exalted is He, is the radiant way that can be found by following God's beloved Prophet. This enlightened way has four gates, one inside the other. These radiant gates are not side by side but within one another.

The first gate is the gate of the Sacred Law (*shari'a*).
The second gate is the gate of the Mystic Path (*tariqa*).
The third gate is the gate of Reality (*haqiqa*).
The fourth gate is the gate of Inner Knowledge (*ma'rifa*).

Beyond the fourth gate lie three palaces, one within the other:

The first palace is that of the Axial Centrality (*qutbiya*).
The second palace is that of Proximity (*qurbiya*).
The third palace is the palace of Devoted Service (*'ubudiya*).

It is not possible to describe with the pen or to define in words the pure delight and divine mysteries concealed herein. Without experience one cannot know, and without experience one cannot be made to understand. There is no conceivable way of showing those who cannot see. Only those who can see, only those who can taste, are capable of attaining this pure delight.

The Sacred Law consists of the sweet words of the noble Messenger. We call it the Speech of the Messenger.

The Mystic Path consists of the exemplary actions of God's beloved Prophet. We call it the Deeds of the Messenger.

Reality consists of the states peculiar to the Prince of the two worlds. We call it the State of the Messenger.

Inner Knowledge consists of the secret of that most holy being, the Mercy to Mankind. We call it the Secrets of Muhammad.

Indeed, those fortunate and blessed individuals who are admitted to this secret attain to purity, gather the roses of the garden of love, and rejoice with the True Beloved. God, Exalted is He, loves them and they love God. This love between the true lover and the true Beloved is a mighty secret incomprehensible to those who have not experienced it.

Sacred Law and Mystic Way lead to the goal. Reality lies deeper, as does Inner Knowledge.

As we have said, the first gate on the way to the Truth is the Sacred Law. But for those with sickness in their hearts, for those who lack the light of faith, this noble Sacred Law of Muhammad is as bitter to the taste as the outer shell of an unripe walnut. Rightly and properly to observe the illustrious Sacred Law, that is, obediently to perform the acts of worship ordained by God, Exalted is He; to do the things He has told us to do, while shunning like the plague those things He has told us not to do; all this weighs heavily upon man's lower self. For instance, the Sacred Law commands us to fast, whereas the lower self would like to eat. The Sacred Law orders us to pray, while the lower self prefers laziness. The Sacred

Law bids us to pay the obligatory Alms, while the lower self thinks it owns whatever it gets and is possessive of its money. The Sacred Law forbids adultery and fornication, whereas the lower self, being the slave of its lust and animal passions, would like to take its pleasure with every beauty it meets.

How could the lower self be fond of the Sacred Law, when this places obstacles in the way of its every desire and inclination? This is why the Sacred Law, the blessed words of God's beloved Prophet, which is really as sweet as honey, tastes as bitter as the outer shell of an unripe walnut to the lower self immersed in its own satisfaction. May not even honey taste bitter to one unaccustomed to the taste of it or to a person who is sick? Thus those whose hearts are sick because of the wickedness of their lower selves, and those who lack the light of faith, find the Sacred Law as bitter as the green outer shell of a walnut.

If we look into the heart of the matter, the Sacred Law is locked in a struggle with the lower self that is much tougher and more savage than any battle waged against the enemies of religion and the nation. Indeed, this is what the Messenger of God, God bless him and give him peace, really meant when he declared that the struggle against external foes constitutes *al-jihad al-asghar* (Lesser Jihad), while the struggle waged with the lower self constitutes *al-jihad al-akbar* (Greater Jihad).

We follow the Halveti way,
to Truth let's up and away,
the Great Campaign we essay,
Imam 'Ali the chief we obey.

The light of the Sacred Law is the beacon tower of guidance. The pearl of the Sacred Law is the crown of happiness. The mystery of the Sacred Law makes the creature who obeys it acceptable to God. The Sacred Law is an elixir whose sweet water restores to life. The

Sacred Law is what makes men human, for the Sacred Law is the light of the Messenger. The full moon of the Sacred Law exposes the evil of worldliness and shows the way to Union. The Sacred Law is the system of each of the two universes; the life of the two worlds is the ocean of the Sacred Law. Confusion is the state of one who lacks the Sacred Law; the sun of the Sacred Law leads to completion. Act in accordance with the Sacred Law, O lover, for it leads to the zenith of success.

The palace of truth is founded on Sacred Law;
The Lord of the way of Truth is the Sacred Law.

This is the door of the convent of Truth,
for the way begins with the Sacred Law.

The ending of these ways is there as well;
The final destination is the Sacred Law.

Calling us to the Path that's Straight,
The herald's cry is the Sacred Law.

The Sacred Law is the Prophet's way;
Guidance for all is the Sacred Law.

On the night of His dear one's Ascension,
God's gift to him was the Sacred Law.

Three years and twenty Gabriel conveyed
God's revelation of the Sacred Law.

The world has sciences of many kinds;
Their cyclopedia is the Sacred Law.

The execution of this unbelieving self,
Such is the judgment of God's Sacred Law.

Those hearty warriors of the Greater War
Refresh their courage in the Sacred Law.

Leading the caravan on its route,
The trusted guide is the Sacred Law.

Reality's the sovereign, true,
But the banner before it is the Sacred Law.

The Sacred Law the saints do not forget;
The friend of saints is the Sacred Law.

The Sacred Law upholds both Heaven and earth;
This building stands upon the Sacred Law.

Of pure law what do atheists know?
That enemy's enemy is the Sacred Law.

Just by their reasoning they know
The height of order is the Sacred Law.

Beware, my friend, don't follow them;
Don't minimize the Sacred Law.

Reality without the Law is atheism;
Reality's light is the Sacred Law.

If its light is not shining, then you will know;
As with Reality, so with the Sacred Law.

No saint comes into this world, unless
He holds in his hand the staff of the Sacred Law.

While his head is crowned with shawl and cloth,
The coat on his back is the Sacred Law.

Reality is the saint's very soul,
On top of his soul there's the Sacred Law.

The soul will depart when the body dies;
The fort of the spirit is the Sacred Law.

You had not decided the soul would cease to be;
Reality's survival is the Sacred Law.

Reality's like an exquisite beauty;
Her golden clothes are the Sacred Law.

By strangers let her not be seen unveiled;
Her modesty and honor is the Sacred Law.

Reality is the Exalted Throne, that's sure;
The equilibrium of that Throne's the Sacred Law.

Of all the Prophets and the saints,
Niyazi's guide is the Sacred Law.

The lower self has four aspects:

The Domineering Self *(al-nafs al-ammara)*
The Censorious Self *(al-nafs al-lawwama)*
The Inspiring Self *(al-nafs al-mulhima)*
The Tranquil Self *(al-nafs al-mutma'inna)*

There is a further grading of the Tranquil Self in three degrees:

The Contented Self *(al-nafs al-radiya)*
The Pleasing Self *(al-nafs al-mardiya)*
The Pure Self *(al-nafs al-safiya)*

When defining the stage of Inner Knowledge, we described these degrees as three different "palaces."

The Domineering Self always leads man to the things forbidden by God, Exalted is He, and keeps him from those He has commanded. This is the self which finds the Sacred Law bitter and hard to bear. Those controlled by this self dislike the Law and try to evade it. This is the self possessed by unbelievers, rebellious sinners, and immoral people. By bringing this self to submission with the sword of the Sacred Law, man gains the upper hand over this great enemy of his; since he is outwardly human, this means that inwardly also he has stepped upon the first rung of the ladder of humanity and begun to climb upwards. If, on the contrary, man lapses into the Domineering Self, he gets lost in an animalistic way of life and may even sink lower than the animal level. Such people may appear superficially human, but inwardly and in essence they are worse than ravenous beasts.

What this means is that it is only the Sacred Law that makes man truly human. With the Lord's help it is possible for those who believe and have faith in God, Exalted is He, and His Chosen Messenger to enter upon this radiant way by the first gate, the gate of the Sacred Law. Then they become engaged in the struggle with the Domineering Self, the Greater Jihad. However, it is one thing to write or talk about doing combat with the Domineering Self, but the action itself is another matter. It is far from easy to see through the many tricks and stratagems of the Domineering Self, combined with the whisperings of the Devil from outside, and to carry on the struggle with the self on one's own.

For instance, traps may be set for the warrior who attempts to apply the precepts of the Sacred Law against his lower self, so that even if he cannot be tempted to abandon his acts of worship, he is lured into nullifying them and sidetracked into the swamps of sanctimoniousness and hypocrisy.

Just look around you! Everybody prays, but can anyone perform his prayers as well as you do? Is there anywhere a servant superior to you? There are plenty of people who neither pray nor keep the Fast. But you not only pray and keep the Fast, but also pay your alms and distribute charity. What creature could excel you in merit? Do not be timid and shy: Let the world know how you perform your service and worship of God; tell everybody how you pray, fast, and pay your alms; make everyone realize what a perfect Muslim you are; tell them all that no one can be better than you! Such tempting suggestions flatter our self-esteem, make us conceited about our piety, seek to infect us with vanity and hypocrisy, envy and intolerance, sensuality and the love of wealth and status. They try their utmost to make us crazy for fame and reputation. Unable to prevent us from worship and obedience, they bid us transgress the prohibitions of God, Exalted is He, and force us to overstep the divine bounds. They do whatever they can to oblige us to commit sins, attempting to lead us astray with suggestions like: "God, Glorified and Exalted is He, is very forgiving and generous; do not be afraid, for He will pardon you too."

Only with the help of the Lord can we be saved from these and other such tricks and ruses of the lower self and the Devil.

Thus we see that those who enter by the gate of the Sacred Law must face many difficulties in order to be able to discern and distinguish whether or not their actions are truly correct. Since they lack the unaided strength to control their own lower selves, they become very confused.

For those who enter by the first gate, the gate of the Sacred Law, and who encounter all the pitfalls, the means of salvation is to have recourse to the second gate, the gate of the Mystic Path, which we have called the Acts of the Messenger. Those who come in by this gate must surrender the control of their lower selves to a perfect spiritual guide. To apply the Sacred Law all on one's own is to be like a sick man attempting his own treatment. When entering by the gate of the Mystic Path, it therefore makes far better sense to leave one's treatment to a skilled and experienced physician. Like a skillful doctor, this perfect spiritual guide will prescribe the correct diet for his patient, specify his medicine and dosages, and see him quickly on the road to health. The perfect spiritual guide heals the wounds opened by the lower self and the Devil, and exerts himself with all means at his disposal to treat and cure the sickness of the self. He strives to rescue his patient from the insinuations, tricks, and stratagems of his lower self and the Devil. Provided the aspirant follows his instructions and recommendations to the letter, his well-being will quickly increase and in addition to this he will easily find the gate of Reality.

It is a precondition of all this, however, that the person who is a guide within the gate of the Mystic Path should be a conscious sheikh, a worthy representative of the most noble Messenger, one whose character is formed on the morality of the Koran and of Muhammad, God bless him and give him peace, who is adorned by and conforms to the praiseworthy Prophetic example, who is conversant with and close to God.

One who appears in the guise of a spiritual director, but who keeps people from worship and obedience and takes the servant away from service, cannot be a perfect spiritual guide. Such devils in the shape of guides are unfortunately innumerable. For the likes of these are indeed the guides of Satan. Do not be shocked at this expression. Just as there are saints who are guides of the All-Merciful, there also exist not a few mad guides of Satan. For the sake of His beloved Prophet, Magnified and Glorified is he, protect us and all mankind from evils like these. Amen, for the sake of the Chief of the Messengers.

Sitting like Satan upon the road leading to the Presence of Oneness, they prevent people from reaching the Truth and, in the name of the way of Truth, lead them astray into the way of error. They are not content with striking at people's faith alone, but even dare to play with their lives, property, honor, and chastity.

My humble advice to travelers on the way of Truth, therefore, is to steer clear of such people, for to keep away from them is to draw close to God, Exalted is He.

The perfect spiritual guide, in the sense intended by us, is upright in all he is and does. He has attained the honor and distinction of being a true and worthy representative of the Greatest Guide, God's beloved Prophet. Possessing the charisma of the being of Muhammad, he expects nothing from anyone but God. He does not himself consume the bounties conferred upon him by God, Exalted is He, but feeds them to others; he does not wear them himself but gives them to others to wear. He is not a hinderer but a helper. He protects his pupils and rescues them from every conceivable and inconceivable kind of evil. He strives to direct them always to the way of Truth. He teaches uprightness, he teaches service to mankind. He inculcates compassion and mercy, as the only means of reaching union with Divine Affection. He does not begrudge or envy his students' hidden talents, but brings them to light by educating them.

Those blessed with the good fortune of being able to meet such a perfect spiritual guide discover the joy and happiness of both Sacred Law and Mystic Path. Reaching the gates of Reality and Inner Knowledge, they pass through to the Palace of Axial Centrality, sit upon the Throne of Proximity, and enjoy the splendor of Divine Service. Those blessed and fortunate beings are annihilated in the Truth and achieve permanence with the Truth. They attain the station of Veracity and reach the Seat of Truthfulness in the sight of God, Magnified and Glorified is He, the All-Powerful King. They enter the Paradise of Essence in the company of the Prophets, the saints and veracious ones, the martyrs and the righteous. They receive Divine bounty and favor. O Allah, make our way easy, for You have the power to ease, O God.

My brother, you faithful lover and seeker after the Truth!

Let me humbly attempt to explain the Sacred Law through the allegory of a rose. When we hold a rose in our hand, the thorn of that rose is the emblem of the Sacred Law, its stem of the Mystic Path, its flower of Reality, and its scent of Inner Knowledge.

The rose can only preserve itself and its scent by means of its thorn and its stem. Without thorn and stem neither rose nor scent would survive. It is these that protect the rose, and in just the same way, Reality and Inner Knowledge are preserved by the Sacred Law and the Mystic Path. Those who want to have the rose and its scent are obliged to put up with the stem and thorn of that rose, but this cannot be considered a great sacrifice on the part of those who love the rose and its perfume. This should never be forgotten. Where the thorn grows there will be a rose. The rose depends for its survival on the thorn. It must be realized that all beginnings are attended by difficulty. On the other hand, the Mighty Proof, the Koran, plainly states that two comforts are granted and bestowed for every hardship.

Can someone who is unable to complete his primary education go on to study in middle school? If he does, will he be able to learn the things he is given to read and understand, and will those who cannot complete this level of education be able to succeed in high school? Will those who cannot finish high school be fit for higher education at university?

The Sacred Law is primary school. The Mystic Path is middle school. Reality may be compared to high school and Inner Knowledge to university.

If the foundations and walls of a building are unsound, its roof will not hold and stay in place. And it is certainly impossible to live in a building without a ceiling. This being so, we may compare the Sacred Law to the foundation of a building, the Mystic Path to its walls, Reality to its roof and ceiling, and Inner Knowledge to its habitability. If these four elements are not combined, we naturally cannot say we have a house.

Can true faith be reached without cutting the girdle of imperfect belief? Can Paradise be arrived at without crossing the sharp and narrow bridge? In other words, unbelief must leave the heart so that faith may come to rest therein.

In order to become a monotheist, a person must be saved from attributing partners to God.

Can a man be born without being deposited as seed in his mother's womb? Can he acquire physical existence? Suppose we compare our mates, our lifelong companions, to the rose, and our mothers-in-law to the thorn: Had it not been for the thorn—in this case our mothers-in-law—how would the rose—in this case our mates—have come into being? In other words, those who want to hold the rose put up with its thorn and accept it gladly as part of nature. It would be a very strange thing indeed for anyone who could not endure the thorn to go looking for the rose.

Those who wish to achieve perfect happiness must be ready for a number of difficulties and hardships, but they should never forget that all problems can be overcome by dint of determination and perseverance.

Furthermore, those who do not know that they must die have no right to live. Those who cannot face the trouble and effort of plowing, sowing, and hoeing their fields cannot possibly take the produce of those fields. Those to whom a woman's suffering is intolerable will not be able to have children and will never know the joys of fatherhood.

One could give many more examples of this kind, but these will surely suffice to make our point. To sum up, let us consider this one final set of comparisons:

What corresponds best to the Sacred Law is that in Islam which the lower self finds difficult and heavy; to the Mystic Path, the benefits accruing from those difficulties; to Reality, being on the way of Truth; to Inner Knowledge, attainment of pure bliss through union with the Truth, and becoming a sovereign in the two worlds.

When the Majesty of Truth was creating and bringing into being Paradise and Hell, He said to Gabriel, on him be peace: "Go and look around the Paradise I have created." Obedient to this Divine command and decree of the All-Glorious, Gabriel, on him be peace, went into Paradise and admired its bounty and degrees, its pavilions and palaces. He was enchanted and amazed.

However, he noticed that there were a number of obstacles to entering Paradise. He understood these to be compulsory religious duties like ablution, washing, prayers, fasting, pilgrimage, alms, and sacred struggle (*jihad*). He made this supplication to the Truth:

"O Lord of all worlds, the Paradise which You have created and brought into existence defies all description. You have created and prepared such bounties as eyes never saw, minds never imagined, and hearts could never even conceive. But hurrah for the creatures who get past these obstacles to reach the bounties. Will any creature ever get through?"

The Almighty deigned to reply:

"There are creatures of Mine so special that they love Me and I also love them. Those creatures of Mine look upon My commands with gratitude as the crown of their good fortune.

"These obstacles can certainly be no barrier to their entering My Paradise. For these creatures of Mine, they may even form a means of entering into My Paradise."

Again by Divine command, Gabriel, on him be peace, went down to Hell. He saw the descending layers of Hell, the chains that were there, the shackles and fetters of fire, the boiling water, the bitter *zaqqum* trees, the snakes as thick as date palms, the scorpions as big as mules, the oceans of fire, and the coffins made of fire. As he trembled in awe of the Divine Majesty, in the throes of terror and dread, he saw that Hell was surrounded with those things dear to the lower self of man, like drink, gambling, women, and other objects desired by the lower self and prepared by Satan as a trap. Once more he asked: "O Lord, have You any creatures who will not be deceived by all these things and who will not enter here?"

The Truth, Glorified and Exalted is He, replied:

"Yes, O Gabriel! My special creatures will never be taken in by this obscenity and filth. They will never depart from My Sacred Law, will never in any way or for any reason neglect My commands and prohibitions. Indeed I have made Hell out of bounds to those special creatures of Mine."

O you who keep faith!

The Mighty Koran is a cure for the believers and the dismay of the unbelievers. The Sacred Law is heavy and difficult for unbelievers and deniers, but for lovers and true believers it is a blessing and good fortune. Yes, to unbelievers, hypocrites, wrongdoers, and sinners the Sacred Law is like April rain. Just as April rain brings fresh new life as a Divine Mercy to the places where it falls, and makes them bloom again, just as it brings vitality, verdure, and beauty to those surroundings, makes the buds in the rose garden open and grow and fills the world with the scent of musk and amber, so does it confer upon true believers the same freshness and vitality, beauty and quality, with the most exquisite perfumes and sensations. In contrast to this, just as that same April rain falling on a garbage dump increases the foul and dirty odors, so does it spread around the nauseating stench of unbelievers, hypocrites, wrongdoers, and sinners. This is why they have no liking at all for the Sacred Law, which is just like April rain.

To believers, the Sacred Law is bounty and good fortune, while to unbelievers it is misfortune and degradation. To believers the Sacred Law is easy and comfortable, while unbelievers and hypocrites find it hard and annoying. To lovers the Sacred Law is light and mercy, while to unbelievers it is a fearful darkness. To believers the Sacred

Law is light and gentle, while to unbelievers it is synonymous with pain and punishment.

Surely that is why, in order to be able to carry out truly and correctly the divine commands which weigh so heavily upon our lower selves, we beg God to make things easy for us, His poor servants, imploring God, Exalted is He, at least forty times a day: "O Lord of all of the Worlds! You alone do we worship, and so that we may always remain in this worship we look to You alone for help." For if Almighty God will not accept one of His servants into His presence, He removes from that servant of His the Sacred Law and the worship and obedience he is obliged to offer to His Divine Essence. That servant cannot derive joy from worship or delight from Remembrance.

The wise say that if a servant misses his prayer at the prescribed time, he should ponder very deeply, asking himself: "I wonder what kind of offense I committed against my Lord, that my Lord did not accept me into His presence." They say that he should repent and seek forgiveness and that he should weep with remorse.

Do not regard these words as odd. God, Magnified and Glorified is He, so loves His believing servants that He condescends to admit them to His presence five times a day. Consequently, those who are thirsty for the love of God should not shun or avoid any sacrifice that will enable them to reach this love. They should surrender to God, Exalted is He, with complete submissiveness, should look upon His commands and decrees with gratitude and regard them as the greatest and most inaccessible happiness for them.

The life of this world is transitory and fleeting. The greatest investment for the permanent and eternal world after this transitory one is faith and faith alone; it is worship, obedience, and love for God, Exalted is He. We came from God and sooner or later we shall return to Him. Therefore those who possess intelligence, conscience, and common sense never let it out of their minds for one moment that He is in every way worthy of being loved, that he is the only true Beloved. They regard His service as the true sovereignty and long to be with Him at every breath. They like the things He likes and dislike the things that He dislikes. They blame what He blames, praise what He praises. They are true to the Truth, know their own selves, live in the love of God, and move on from this transitory world to the everlasting world as lovers of the Truth. These blessed and fortunate beings are undying. That is, they do not remain unrealized.

Thus the Mystic Path leads nowhere without the Sacred Law, while the Sacred Law without the Mystic Path is abandoned to disbelievers and hypocrites. To lovers the Sacred Law is sweeter than honey; to the thirsty the Mystic Path is more delicious than pure cool water. Reality is a crown and Inner Knowledge an everlasting sovereignty, which never passes away. Without the Sacred Law and without the Mystic Path, Reality and Inner Knowledge are accessible only through the grace, favor, and guidance of God, Exalted is He. For God, Glorified and Exalted is He, is absolute master in His domain, with power to bestow what He will upon whom He will. He guides aright whomever He wishes and allows whomever He wishes to go astray. He punishes whomever He wishes, and whomever He wishes He gladdens with His pardon. Paradise and the Divine Beauty are attained not through acts of worship, but only by His grace. If He wishes, He may pardon all things except the sin of attributing partners to Him. He is forgiving and loves forgiveness. He is generous and loves generosity. He comes running to those who walk toward Him. He remembers those who remember His Divine Essence. He is All-Merciful and does not desert those who recognize His Essence of Oneness. He is slow to punish but never neglectful. He is kind and loves kindness. He is beautiful and loves the beautiful. He does not desert, sadden, or cut off any who call "Allah!" Those who love Him must also love those dear to Him, the chief of whom is His beloved Prophet, our master Muhammad the Chosen, God bless him and give him peace. God, Magnified and

Exalted is He, has graciously condescended to make plain to those who love His Divine Essence the honor and respect enjoyed in His Exalted sight by His Messenger, God bless him and give him peace. For the All-Glorious ordered: "If you love Me and are sincere in this love of yours, then follow Muhammad and love him so that I may also love you and may pardon your sins."

O seeker after the Truth!

To be able to learn the Sacred Law of Islam, it is your duty first of all to learn the meaning and nature of the doctrines and acts of worship of the clear religion of Islam, then to learn the truth of Islamic Sufism and to practice all you have learned with complete sincerity.

Those who wish to be able to attain Reality and to experience Inner Knowledge of the self, by obediently worshipping God, Exalted is He, with this sincerity, absolutely must submit to the instruction and training of a perfect spiritual guide. They must give up the bad and unclean qualities of the lower self, which are vanity, pride, hypocrisy, egoism, and self-centeredness. They must cultivate a character modeled on the morality of the Koran, cast out from their hearts anything other than the love of God and the affection of the Messenger, strip themselves clean of "all but," enlighten and beautify their hearts with the love of God, and the affection of God's Messenger.

If seekers of the Truth are able to practice this honesty and sincerity, they will soon attain their goal.

One of the most necessary and important duties for lovers is to treat with affection the people of God. For since affection for the people of God is identical with affection for God's Messenger, and since affection for God's Messenger is affection for God Most High, it is a cause and means of increasing a person's success.

Lovers' success is most enhanced by affection for their spiritual guide, by loving performance of their service to him, and by prayers and endeavors for the most worthy being. Affection for the guide, arising from deep within the pupil, is like the spiritual river flowing in the inner being of the guide. Indeed, this abundant flow causes the bounty of the spiritual guide to spill over to his pupil. Thus the current of this bounty ebbs or flows according to the pupil's affection for his guide. In short, the pupil should love his guide with a genuine, sincere, and unhypocritical affection. It should be well understood that there is a path from heart to heart. Consequently, the pupil is recompensed for his love and affection toward his guide by the blessing he experiences from him and rapidly approaches his goal. For all that we have explained has stood the test of centuries and constitutes the essence of truths that have been seen to yield positive and fruitful results.

THE JEWELS IN THE CHEST

8

THE SPIRITUAL GUIDE

These duties, to be observed in respect of the spiritual guide, must be known and committed to memory:

1. Good habits associated with purity of intention: In order to earn God's pleasure the lover must carefully control his hand, his sex, and his tongue.

2. Good habits associated with the connecting Bond: The lover must never let the Sheikh out of his mind. In the absence of his Sheikh he must observe the same good conduct as if he were in the Sheikh's presence. He must not fall short in loving service to his Sheikh and must behave as if the Sheikh were there.

3. In the presence of his spiritual guide he must pay extraordinary attention to the way he conducts himself.

4. In speaking with his Sheikh he must be extremely polite, well mannered in his words and behavior. If notice is taken of him, he should not let this go to his head, nor should he take offense if he receives an admonition.

5. He should regard it as a privilege to be able to serve the spiritual guide with faithful devotion.

6. He must be polite when requesting of his Sheikh the gift of sincerity, material or spiritual benefit, and inner peace.

7. He must behave with the utmost propriety while reciting his set passages of Scripture and Remembrances.

8. While engaged in spiritual exercises and struggle with the lower self, he must be extremely careful to behave correctly.

As we have said, the first duty is to behave with purity of intention. It should never be forgotten that every deed and every action is judged according to the intention behind it. Therefore whatever the lover does, whatever action he performs, must be done for the sake of God. Actions performed with complete sincerity and for God's sake are accepted and approved. But deeds that are done to be seen by creatures and to win their praise and love may be adulterated with hypocrisy. Actions performed with the intention of winning the good pleasure of the Truth, and for the sake of God, are accepted and rewarded by God, Exalted is He. Actions performed to be seen by others, and more or less mixed with hypocrisy, may perhaps attract some human esteem, but the ostentatious hypocrite cannot benefit in the Hereafter. Those who work for worldly ends may gain the world and acquire everything they want. But he who works for the sake of the Hereafter will receive the reward of the Hereafter. Those who are grateful to Almighty God soon find and take their certain recompense. This truth is stated in the Mighty Proof, the Koran. Therefore those who seek the Truth and God's good pleasure should do whatever they do with the genuine intention of pleasing Him.

The second duty is conduct befitting the connecting Bond. For the sake of God, the sincere pupil in God's way should direct his heart with the help of his Sheikh toward the Divine Majesty. He should seek only God, Exalted is He, and to please the Truth. Neither this world nor the Next should he seek, but God Himself, Glorified and Exalted is He, crying: "My Guide, You are my goal. Your noble pleasure is all I desire and wish." As the lover leaves Names in quest of the Named—or, in other words, as the pupil seeks the

Essence—it is not proper for him to address himself to the attributes. To turn toward the Essence, to seek the Essence, is certainly much higher in degree than turning toward the attributes. Those who seek God's Essence cannot and must not seek either this world or the Hereafter. For their sole aim is the Essence. The Essence is undoubtedly far more exalted than the attributes. Besides, he who possesses the Essence is bound to possess the attributes. He who possesses the attributes, on the other hand, cannot possess the Essence.

The third duty of the pupil is to behave correctly in the presence of his spiritual guide. In the absence of the Sheikh, the pupil should conduct himself exactly as he would in the Sheikh's presence, should perform his duties fully, and should be extremely polite and well behaved everywhere and in all that he does. The belief and conviction that, although we cannot see Almighty God, He sees us however we are and whatever we are doing, transforms a creature's submission into active goodness and brings him to the condition of perfect belief. The knowledge that God, Exalted is He, is nearer to him than his own arteries increases the love and longing in the pupil's heart for the journey to God. The only goal is God, Lord of Majesty and Perfection. For those linked with the Sheikh by such a bond, this connection is an aid to their journey to God. A perfect and mature pupil must have the highest affection for the person of his guide, for his deeds, and for his obedience to the Truth. The spiritual influence of the guide will most certainly never leave the heart of a pupil who succeeds in this. How could there be a separation when a person can never forget the one he truly loves? His mind, thoughts, and memory are all upon his Beloved. So if a sincere pupil approaches his spiritual guide with the respect and affection due to him, he will always have the company of his Sheikh upon his spiritual journey and will not let him out of his mind for one instant. Thanks to the bounty and blessings he will enjoy in this state, the faithful pupil will easily attain the good pleasure of the Truth. To be completely committed to the belief that this absolutely must be so is called the Bond. The respect and affection in which the faithful pupil holds his guide is such that it makes him forget himself, though he never ceases to be aware of his guide. At this level the duality of guide and pupil disappears and the pupil is annihilated in his guide. The degree of Annihilation in the Sheikh resulting from this sincerity of the pupil toward his guide is bestowed by God, Exalted is He, as a great favor upon faithful pupils. The Divine success attained by the guide then begins to be acquired by the pupil also. This is a most enormous blessing from the Lord. Four high degrees are divinely conferred upon the pupil privileged to attain such blessedness:

The degree of Annihilation in the Sheikh
The degree of Annihilation in the Founding Saint of the Order
The degree of Annihilation in the Messenger
The supreme benefaction of Annihilation in God

Those who are annihilated in God, Exalted is He, and become immortal with the Truth, rejoice with Him and attain the Seat of Veracity.

For the pupil who wishes to serve his guide, it is absolutely necessary that he be in a state of ritual ablution. This ablution must be both external and internal. The four obligatory elements of ritual ablution are: washing the hands and arms up to the elbows, washing the face, wiping one-fourth of the head, and washing the feet up to the ankles. The following are optional but recommended: rinsing the mouth and nose after washing the hands, combing the beard with the fingers while washing the face, and washing three times each of the mentioned parts of the body except for the head.

As for the internal ablution, lovers who wish to serve the spiritual guide must devote to it the same care and attention as to the external ablution we have just described. Exactly as the external ablution removes the dirt from the hands, arms, face, feet, etc., the internal ablution purifies and cleanses all these parts of the body of spiritual dirt. While the physical dirt adhering to the hand, for instance, can be cleaned away by washing with water, water is not effective in removing spiritual dirt. This is why, in places where water is unavailable, the act of *tayammum* (wiping with sand or clean topsoil) has been made obligatory, as a pointer to inner cleanliness and to emphasize the value and importance of internal ablution. Consequently, when lovers come to take their external ablution, they should think of these things while pronouncing the noble formula BISMI-LLAHI-L-RAHMANI-L-RAHIM (In the name of God, All-Merciful, All-Compassionate), declare their intention, and address God, Exalted is He, in the following words:

> My God, I shall not reach out my hand where it will incur Your noble displeasure. I shall not open my hand to beg from any but Your Divine Essence. If since the last time I took ablution I have unwittingly, mistakenly, or absent-mindedly put my hand to anything displeasing to You, as I clean these hands of mine by washing them with water, so let me also keep spiritually clean.

Rubbing between the fingers signifies symbolically washing one's hands of the love of this world. While rinsing out the mouth three times in accordance with the recommended practice, by way of internal ablution one should think about these things and address the following supplication to Almighty God:

> O Lord, with this mouth I have remembered Your Divine Essence, proclaimed Your Unity, recited Your Book, and uttered thanks and praise to You. I shall not use it for backbiting, telling lies, speaking wicked and dirty words, or pronouncing falsehoods against others. I shall not befoul it with unnecessary, empty, and

meaningless words, unbelief, vituperation, and abuse. By Your grace, let no such words displeasing to You leave this mouth of mine, and grant me only such things as are good and lawful in conformity with Your noble pleasure.

As the mouth is washed and cleaned externally with water—with the frayed end of the stick called *miswak,* or with toothbrush and paste, or, if none of these are available, by rubbing with the finger—so the inner ablution is performed by thinking of the matters mentioned above and by declaring one's intention. It thus becomes possible to avoid and beware of things forbidden by God, Exalted is He, and so to ensure the inner and spiritual cleanliness of the mouth.

Similarly, when rinsing the nose three times one should pray:

My God, let my nose smell the scents of Paradise, the fragrant perfume of Muhammad.

And while washing the face:

O Lord, I turn my face to none but Your Divine Essence, I beg of none but You, and of You is my only expectation. Your Divine Approval is all I seek. Grant to my eyes the sight of Your blessed instruction. May I behold only the blessings of Your Paradise and Your Perfect Beauty. When that dread day comes, on which the faces of the unbelievers will be gloomy and their eyes made blank, make my face bright, do not wipe from my brow the mark of prostration, let my countenance shine with the light of the Koran and the radiance of the All-Merciful's Beloved, and as You made this ordinary face of mine human, make my inner and spiritual face human also.

Evidence to confirm the view we have expressed is found in the noble Koranic verse prescribing ablution as a religious obligation.

This is what God, Magnified and Glorified is He, says in His Noble Koran:

"O believers, when it is time for you to perform the Prayer, wash your hands and your face . . . ."

This means that human beings have both an outer and an inner face, which is why the Glorious Divine Command uses the plural forms "hands" and "faces," rather than the singular "hand" and "face."

Yes, we should be conscious of this by way of internal ablution while washing our arms in the external one. And we should make this humble supplication and declaration of intent:

> My God, let my arms not act in contravention of Your Divine Pleasure. For Your sake alone let them hold, for You let them write, for You let them work, for Your Noble Approval let them strike. I shall not use my hands and arms for evil ends; I shall not write evil things; I shall not injure anyone by striking him down without just cause. Moreover, I pray that I may receive the record of my deeds from the right and in my right hand, and that my wrists be not shackled and thrust into Hellfire.

Likewise, while wiping the head:

> My God, You have crowned my head with true faith. Never take that mighty crown from my head nor cast me among the faithless mob.

When going on to wet the back of the neck and the ears:

> O Lord, let my ears hear only the words of Truth; let me not listen to speech displeasing to You. As You have most graciously addressed me in this world with "O believer!," let me rejoice in this noble appellation on the coming Day of Resurrection. Do not

burden with unbelief and hypocrisy this neck of mine, which You have laden with the privilege and honor of servitude. Do not charge it with the load of sin and rebelliousness. Do not set upon my neck the yoke and chains of Hell.

Finally, while washing the feet:

O Lord, set these feet of mine firmly and constantly upon the ways of right guidance. Let my feet never stray from the path that leads to Your Divine Pleasure, Your Approval, Your Paradise, and Your Beauty. Enable me to walk till my last breath along the Straight Path. I promise not to go where Your Noble Pleasure is lacking, but always and everywhere to make my way directly toward Your Divine Approval only.

Lovers who carry out all this precisely and to the letter while taking their external ablution will at the same time have performed their internal ablution: They will have combined and completed both together. Those who begin their ablution with BISMI-LLAHI-L-RAHMANI-L-RAHIM, and end it with AL-HAMDU LILLAH (To God belongs the praise), and who repeat the Affirmation of Divine Unity and Profession of Faith as they wash each part of the body, will have made a perfect ablution both inwardly and outwardly, conforming to the Noble Pleasure of God, Exalted is He. Such is the ablution of the lovers. The formally pious make their ablution with water alone, and they will surely be rewarded. As for the lovers, as they make their ablution both outwardly and inwardly, mingling their tears with the water, since they have washed with tears heated even to the boiling point by the fire of love in their hearts, they are in the presence of the King, enraptured, intoxicated, and lost in wonder.

This is why lovers seeking the Truth are reminded and instructed by their spiritual guides that they must always keep themselves in a state of ablution. They advise and teach their pupils to be faultless in these ablutions of theirs. In any case, to keep oneself constantly in a state of ritual purity is recommended in the illustrious Sacred Law. But in the Mystic Path of Muhammad it is necessary and compulsory in obedience to the guide's command. For those who wish to serve the Sheikh, therefore, being in a constant state of ablution is a prerequisite. There are innumerable advantages to keeping oneself in this condition. It means that one is ever ready and prepared for worship. Besides, it is a happy fact that those who are constantly in a state of ablution will not be afflicted with apoplexy.

The lover should always repent for his sins, shortcomings, and carelessness. At the same time, he should also seek forgiveness for all the believers. Seeking forgiveness means saying: "O Lord, I beg you to pardon and forgive me."

The lover should make a gift to the spirit of his guide by reciting the glorious Sura *al-Fatiha* and the noble Sura *al-lkhlas*. The lover must always bind his heart to the heart of his guide, and in this bond he should he completely sincere and affectionate. For there is a path from heart to heart. Because of the pupil's perfect affection for his guide, he should know for certain that his guide's spiritual influence is with him wherever he may be. For whether the faithful pupil be awake, asleep, or dreaming, the spirit of his guide is never apart from him. The people of Reality are unanimously agreed that, since the spiritual guide is the means whereby the sincere pupil attains his object and station, if the pupil lets his guide out of his awareness for a split second, if he forgets him as long as it takes to bat an eyelid, that pupil cannot be accepted as a sincere seeker of the Truth.

The faithful pupil should serve his guide without looking him in the face. He should think of the Sheikh's presence as a fortress and behave as meekly toward his Sheikh as if he were a fugitive who had been recaptured after having fled the service of the king. He should not sit down in his presence unless told to do so by his guide, If he has some problem of Sacred Law or Jurisprudence, or relating to the Mystic Path, he must ask about it with polite respect and seek the solution to his problem. He should not say one word about himself, and in the presence of his Sheikh he should never converse with his brothers. However old or senior in the order he may be, he should still avoid talking in the guide's presence. For loud conversation in the Sheikh's presence, with the brethren or others, may be an obstacle to the pupil's progress, opening the way to his failure and disappointment.

There are many advantages to abstaining from talk in the presence of the spiritual guide. Two specific examples are (1) honor and respect for the Sheikh and his position, and (2) self-effacement.

Just as a person in love never takes his eyes off his loved one, the pupil in the presence of his guide should have the attitude of a lover toward his beloved. He must pay no attention to the people sitting with the Sheikh, but should rather increase his respect, affection, and reverence toward his guide. Since the pupil's respect, affection, love, and reverence for the guide are all for the sake of God and His Messenger, what is apparently for the Sheikh is actually directed toward God, Exalted is He, and His Chosen Messenger. It is therefore necessary to remain calm and humble in the Sheikh's presence, to supplicate for the attainment of one's goal and the satisfaction of one's desire, and to be inwardly resigned.

Since the faithful pupil recognizes his guide as the representative and vicegerent of God's Messenger, God bless him and give him peace, he must never forget that respect and obedience to the guide are in effect respect and obedience to God's beloved Messenger, while disobedience to the guide is actually rebellion against the noble Messenger and Almighty God Himself. In fact, this is stated in a noble Hadith, which should be beard by all the heedless. The sense of it is as follows:

"To obey me is to obey God, Exalted is He. To disobey me is to disobey God, the Lord of Glory and Perfection. To obey your commander is to obey me. To disobey your commander is to disobey me."

The learned are the heirs of the Prophets. Another noble Hadith tells us: "The learned among my people is like a Prophet amid his Community."

According to yet another noble Hadith: "The learned of my Community are like the Prophets of the Children of Israel."

Clearly, then, the sincere reverence accorded to their guides by the dervish fraternity is the cause of their advancement and elevation. On the other side of the coin, to despise and belittle the guide is the cause of their retrogression on the Mystic Path. Thus heedlessness of heart in the presence of the Sheikh or opposition to him, looking down upon the Sheikh or behaving toward him in an offhand manner, since they alienate the guide from the pupil concerned, result in his losing the guide's regard and affection. The people of Truth have said:

"A fall of seven floors is a gentle drop compared with falling from the heart and affection of the spiritual guide."

Anyone who speaks sweetly and reasonably, to please God and from respect for his Sheikh and teacher, will be forgiven and will enjoy success and salvation.

One should not pretend to agree with the words of the guide, while actually or in one's heart contradicting him. For the pupil who opposes and contradicts the guide, whether literally or in his heart, can never find deliverance. This is because the people of God sometimes have in them an importance and power that stems from Pure Power. There is also weight and power based on wisdom. To question an action of the guide and to query its cause and motive, to oppose and contradict the Sheikh even in one's heart, to dare to quarrel and object, these things constitute such improper conduct toward that most holy being, that they threaten to destroy the pupil responsible for such foul and wicked behavior.

It must never be forgotten that the will of the guide lies not in himself but in the Truth. His actions cannot all be taken at face value, as they have many hidden causes and motives. One should therefore be totally accepting, still one's heart, keep silent, and say nothing.

O seeker after Truth!

As we have said, it is absolutely impermissible on the Mystic Path to speak with the guide in an informal manner. This is allowed only when necessary to the urgent solution of some religious or worldly problem. After relating a dream one has seen or a spiritual revelation one has had the blessing to receive, one should wait and then listen with all one's attention if the guide gives an interpretation. If he gives none, one should on no account press him insistently. One should accept that there must be a good reason for the Sheikh's silence.

As we have mentioned, the fifth rule to be observed in respect of the guide is that of service to him. This service may be either physical or financial.

Service to the spiritual guide must be performed in the belief that it is ultimately for God and His Messenger and in the knowledge that it is a great and blessed favor from God, Exalted is He.

One should be pleased and grateful for the privilege of being able to serve. The task one is given should not be resented or carried out reluctantly; otherwise the spiritual benefit will be lost. He who works and serves for the sake of God is sure to be rewarded. In this service, the Sheikh's requests should be treated as commands to be acted upon at once without delay, no matter how difficult the task may be. The Sacred Law, however, does not permit compliance with a command when such compliance would entail—God forbid—an act of disobedience to God, Exalted is He, since it cannot be lawful to obey a creature in disobedience to Almighty God. But on the Mystic Path the pupil is nevertheless obliged to obey his Sheikh, for he must expect to be tested by his guide and must trust his good intention. The pupil's firm conviction will cause him to reflect:

"My guide would certainly never wish me to disobey God, Exalted is He. What he has told me to do, though apparently in conflict with the Sacred Law, is surely based upon some hidden wisdom."

Perfect guides have in fact been known to test and reform their pupils by setting them apparently unlawful tasks in the course of their spiritual training. These matters are comprehensible only to people of mature understanding.

There was once a pupil who was afflicted with the disease of sanctimonious pride. In order to correct this defect in his character, his Sheikh made him break his Ramadan fast in daytime and in public, knowing that this would expose the pupil to opprobrium and render him liable to imprisonment according to the letter of the Sacred Law. When Ramadan was over, he made that same pupil fast for sixty days in succession as penance, and one additional day to make up for the one on which he had broken fast. There are countless perfect guides like this one, hidden from common view.

The day had come when a certain conscious guide, a most saintly being conversant with God, was about to leave for the eternal world. He wished to inform his pupils of the stations they had attained, to let them know their degrees of submissiveness to the Sheikh and to indicate which of his lieutenants was most worthy to succeed him. He therefore summoned them all and said to each one: "I order you to bring your wife to my room tonight." Although they all obediently replied: "So be it, Efendi," they regarded this as an unlawful command. Thinking to themselves, "How can we be expected to perform such a disgusting and unlawful task?," they reproached their Sheikh and decided to ignore his command. For the task they had been set was to all appearances in contravention of the noble Sacred Law and constituted flagrant disobedience to God, Exalted is He. To obey a creature in a matter like this was therefore impermissible.

However, one of their number was a man of genuine wisdom. He thought to himself: "In all the many years I have obeyed and served my Sheikh, he has never once set us any task at variance with the Rules of the Sacred Law, Islam, humanity, or morality. There must certainly be some hidden wisdom in all this, as yet incomprehensible to us. I have complete confidence in my Sheikh."

He thereupon went home to fetch his wife and brought her to the Sheikh's room. The Sheikh sent him downstairs to light the stove and boil water, saying that he was going to perform total ablution. The Sheikh got into bed and said to his lieutenant's wife: "My daughter, I am on the point of breathing my last. I am about to meet my Lord. When I yield up my spirit, just bind my chin and my toes, place something heavy upon my belly, and grant me your forgiveness. As soon as he had said this, he gave a cry of "Allah" and surrendered his spirit.

Weeping and wailing, the poor woman ran downstairs to give the news to her husband, who was busy lighting the stove and boiling water. Having proved himself truly sincere in submission to his spiritual guide, he was unanimously accepted as his Sheikh's successor.

We have given these examples to show how some things that happen on the Mystic Path, while apparently in conflict with the Sacred Law, are really in complete conformity with it. Through these and many similar occurrences, many who were previously unaware have discovered the meaning of these mysteries and become conversant with God. By being in the hands of his guide like a corpse in the hands of a washer of the dead, the pupil ensures his ascending progress. Perfect guides are the skilled physicians of the spirit. For those who wish to become mature human beings under the aegis of their training and treatment, it is essential to submit to them with total submissiveness. Great wisdom lies in their every order and instruction. Those who wish to reach their goal must carry out the orders of their guide, even if they cannot comprehend the underlying reasons for them. Those who object or go against them, supposing them to be unlawful, are doomed to immaturity.

As we mentioned above, struggle with the lower self is the Greater Jihad. Only mature men are fit for this struggle. War is strategy, and not everyone can grasp the strategy of the lower self and the Devil. But those who are skilled in combat with these foes can sometimes trick the Devil himself through simulated disobedience into obeying God, beating the Devil at his own game and leaving him dumbfounded. There are numerous tales to support this assertion, but we have no space for them here.

Whenever the pupil has made a promise to his guide, he is absolutely committed to fulfill his undertaking even if he knows himself to be at death's door. He must set all his own affairs aside till he has discharged his promise, and must not postpone it one instant from the time appointed by his guide.

The proper way to render material or financial service to the Sheikh is as follows:

The pupil must be convinced that all the wealth and children bestowed on him by God, Exalted is He, have been graciously conferred as a Divine Favor through the spiritual influence of his guide in the Eternal World. He should therefore regard his wealth and children as belonging entirely to his guide. He must see himself as the slave of his Sheikh and be conscious that his food, drink, and clothing come to him through the generosity of his guide. If he has something to present to his guide, he should not give it publicly but should send it or have it conveyed by someone serving in the Sheikh's household. He should feel gratitude if his offering is accepted by his guide, and should thank God, Exalted is He, that it has not been rejected by the Sheikh.

As we tried to explain earlier, the pupil must recognize and acknowledge his guide as the representative and vicegerent of God's Messenger, God bless him and give him peace. Therefore, if the guide rejects him, he must believe that God and His Messenger have rejected him too, while the guide's acceptance means their acceptance also.

The pupil must always be respectful toward his Sheikh and even in his sleep should not stretch his legs rudely in bed, for he should believe that the spirit of his guide is ever-present and watchful over him, and is informed with the consent of God, Exalted is He, of his every move and step. He must in all circumstances treat his guide with respect and affection, and should be fearful and anxious about losing that respect and affection. He should be well aware that the perfect guide, whether in this life or in the Eternal World, is ready with his spiritual influence to rescue his pupil even at the point of death from the evil wiles of Satan and to drive off the Devil at once. The spirit of the guide is at the pupil's side as he faces the questions of the angels Munkar and Nakir in the grave, and helps him as he answers them. Even in the grave he protects him and saves him from the evil tricks and stratagems of Satan. The Devil always flees from the spiritual influence of the guide.

Come, brother, if it's the Truth you seek,
There's only one way—through a perfect guide.
If it's the Messenger's beauty you seek,
There's only one way—through a perfect guide.

Many have come with the guide as their quest;
When they found him, he soon put their troubles to rest.
A millennium of reading you may try to digest;
There's only one way—through a perfect guide.

Come now, brothers, come, let's go,
Lovers' hearts will overflow;
Gabriel did Muhammad show,
There's one way only—through a perfect guide.

Judges, lawyers, quite a throng,
Asking us, their books among,

"Whom did you get your knowledge from?"
There's one way only—through a perfect guide.

Spread all the books out if you care to,
Read all that's in them if you care to,
Interpret every letter if you dare to;
There's only one way—through a perfect guide.

There's sense in this, Yunus Emre said,
Go to your perfect guide, he said,
Go to Moses and Khidr, he said,
There's only one way—through a perfect guide.

O faithful lover!

Be well aware that spiritual power is unconstrained by space or time. Some wise men have related the following:

"As some of our brothers were approaching the tomb of a fellow pupil who was close to God, there was revealed to them a vision in which they saw the spirit of the perfect guide coming to the aid of his pupil, consoling him and assuaging him of the terror and loneliness of the grave."

Such occurrences must be ascribed to the Power of God, for belief in the infinite Power and Strength of God, Exalted is He, is fundamental to true faith. In spiritual matters like this, since the mind is out of its depth, simple acceptance is called for. These are all Divine Mysteries. It is self-evident that Divine Secrets are beyond the scope of human reason. A really intelligent person is one who believes with conviction that the perfect guide is conscious of him and observes him, by Divine leave, whatever he is doing and whatever his condition—even when not physically present with him. Only God, Glorified and Exalted is He, knows the Unseen World, but He also gives knowledge of it to whom He wills among His servants.

The pupil should therefore place no reliance upon his wealth and property, rank and status, life and health. He should hold these of no account and should rely exclusively upon the munificent generosity of Almighty God.

No material possessions can compare to the bountiful munificence of God, Exalted is He. We should never forget that this is the source of all our blessings.

9

ADVICE TO THE LOVER

Defects of character displeasing to God and His chosen Messenger are to be avoided. Among these are arrogance, hypocrisy, sanctimonious pride, reputation-seeking, envy, irascibility, sensuality, material greed, and status-seeking.

Arrogance (kibr) means thinking oneself superior to others, indifference to the truth, puffing oneself up and "acting big."

Hypocrisy (riya') means doing good and admirable deeds, not to please God, but as a show to win approval and applause. The ostentatious hypocrite is called *mura'i.*

Sanctimonious pride ('ujb) is considering oneself more pious than others, self-righteous vanity, a supercilious attitude to the devotions of others and overconfidence about one's own.

Reputation-seeking (sum'a) means behaving admirably, not with the intention of earning God's approval, but in the hope of attracting attention and acquiring fame and popularity as a good man.

Envy (hasad) is the condition of one who feels jealous resentment toward the merits of others and the blessings attained by them, and who has no qualms about trying to undo them. Such a person is called *hasid.* The simple desire to possess the same blessings as others is termed *ghibta,* or envy free of malice. While this is permissible in the Sacred Law, it is quite unacceptable in the Mystic Path and Reality.

Irascibility (ghadab) is the tendency to be hot-tempered and fly into a rage over every little thing, behaving badly in all kinds of ways while in this impetuous state. Irascibility—quickness to anger—is a very nasty defect of character, and one that can destroy a person spiritually and materially.

Sensuality (shahwa) is enslavement to the lower self, a craving for things forbidden by God, the ruthless and unscrupulous pursuit of one's ambitions, putting the fulfillment of selfish wishes and desires before the commandments and decrees of God, Exalted is He. Those who have the misfortune to be addicted to their sensual lusts are content to sacrifice their all in pursuit of their desires, with no thought for the Day of Resurrection, heedless of where they come from and regardless of right and wrong.

Material greed (hubb al-mal) is an attribute of those who may be called worldly or materialistic. Such people empty their hearts of all other affection and fill them with love of wealth and the things of this world. They soil their hearts, which should be the place of Divine vision.

Status-seeking (hubb al-jah) is the pursuit of rank and status. Those addicted to it will stop at no wickedness, consider no sacrifice too great, to achieve their ambitions. Alas, we see all too many examples of this in every country of today's world.

All these characteristics are attributes of the Devil. We must strive to rid ourselves of them by transforming arrogance into modesty and humility; hypocrisy into sincerity; sanctimony into dissatisfaction with our accomplishments; self-reliance into reliance on God. We must ensure that our good works are performed, not for fame, but for the Truth alone. Envy must yield to gratitude and contentment with what God has given us. A hot temper must give way to mildness and docility. Sensual lust and selfish desire must be subordinated to the wishes and commandments of God, Exalted is He.

Love of material and worldly things must be turned into love of God and His Messenger. The ruthless quest for rank and status must be replaced by the honor and dignity of service to the Truth. There is no other salvation from these bad qualities and the perils and injuries to which they give rise. As for those who cannot cleanse and purify themselves of these foul Satanic attributes, they can never become dervishes or even be considered true believers and Muslims.

One of the practices of the Mystic Way is to spend time in retreat, away from other people, repenting for one's misdeeds and tearfully imploring the pardon and forgiveness of God, Exalted is He.

At every opportunity the lover should beg God, Glorified and Exalted is He, to keep him steadfast upon the Straight Path. At the same time, he should pray for the health and well-being of his guide, for his elevation in spiritual degree, to share his guide's success in promoting the cause of the Sacred Law and Mystic Path and in reviving the praiseworthy example of God's Chosen Prophet, and that he may die a true believer. He must also recite the glorious Sura *al-Fatiha* and the noble Sura *al-lkhlas* for the sake of the soul, blessed with revelations, of the founding saint of the order. He must pronounce benedictions upon the Prophet, God bless him and give him peace.

After this, he should close his eyes and think of himself as having died. They have stripped his corpse, laid it on the bench, washed it and wrapped it in the shroud, prayed over it, and put it to rest in the grave. He should reflect on each stage in this process, for this meditation, which we call *tazakkur al-mawt* (recollecting death), is one of the practices of the Mystic Orders. To ponder one's death is not to cause it, but it is harmful to avoid the thought of death. For no one can or will escape the sure and destined end that comes sooner or later to every mortal being, namely death. This meditation is therefore an essential necessity for every lover who believes his guide to be with him always and everywhere as he seeks the Truth, Exalted is He, praying: "My God, You are my goal; all I desire is Your noble pleasure," and who turns to and clings to the spirit of his guide as he moves with him and through him toward union with God, Exalted is He.

Those who attach themselves in this manner to the Gate of God will certainly not be turned away empty-handed from that door. It should be known for a certainty that those who cleanse their hearts of worldly cares and worries as they stand at the Divine Gate, who proclaim the Unity of the Truth with every breath, who first purify their hearts and rid them of the sin of association with LA ILAHA, then confirm and reassure them with ILLA-LLAH, who thus remember the Exalted Lord, they shall be remembered in turn by the Lord of All Worlds and shall achieve union through the mutual remembrance of rememberer and Remembered by the Grace and Mercy of the All-Glorious. The rememberer then begins with the Name of Majesty, saying: ALLAH, ALLAH . . . . He is honored with the response of the Lord of the Worlds: "At your service, at your service *(Labbayk, labbayk)*, my servant!" As he now continues with the Name of Essence: HU . . . HU . . . HU . . . , he completes his union, and with this completion Remembrance begins. In fact there is no end to Remembrance, for the end of Remembrance is the beginning of Remembrance. This condition is bound up with the exhilaration of the rememberer. The longer he remains in this state, the greater his euphoria and delight. If he stays immersed in it night and day, it becomes an incentive to progress and an occasion of mercy for the lover.

Therefore the lover must never forget the Lord, be he standing, sitting, or lying down. He must remember the Lord of the Worlds openly or secretly, by night or by day, with the tongue or in the heart, publicly and privately. His heart must never be devoid of Remembrance.

While the lover is engaged in Divine Remembrance with his tongue and in the depths of his heart, observing upon his heart the Word of Majesty and the Divine Manifestation, he may find himself in a condition where his lips are sealed, his tongue cleaves to his palate, and with his heart alone he begins spontaneously to call ALLAH . . . ALLAH. In Sufi parlance, such Remembrance is called *walad al-qalb* (the child of the heart).

In telling the praises of God, attention must be paid to the number of repetitions made. Thus it is necessary to make Remembrance at least five thousand times in a day and a night, that is, every twenty-four hours. The more this number is exceeded, the better. If one repeats ALLAH a thousand times after each of the five prescribed prayers, that makes five thousand in a day. It is an important daily duty for everyone who treads the Path to affirm the Divine Unity at least seven hundred times, to utter the Name of Majesty (ALLAH) five hundred times and the Name of Essence (HU) five hundred times. Those who wish to progress more rapidly toward union ought to recite at least seven hundred Affirmations of Unity, followed by five thousand Names of Majesty and five hundred Names of Essence. Those who are able to practice this will quickly attain union. This advice is general. There are exceptional cases, for the Mercy of God, Exalted is He, is all-encompassing.

Another important piece of advice is this:

If a worldly notion enters the heart during Remembrance, one should say: "My God, You are my goal; all I desire is Your noble pleasure." Before beginning Remembrance, one should always repeat ASTAGHFIRU-LLAH at least fifteen, otherwise twenty, seventy, or one hundred times. This means: "My God, pardon me; I beg Your pardon and forgiveness." Both before and after the dhikr, a means of ensuring its acceptance in the sight of God is to recite benedictions upon the Most Noble Messenger, God bless him and give him peace, at least fifteen or twenty-five times.

God's beloved Messenger said: "When a creature begins proclaiming the Divine Unity, the Throne of the All-Merciful starts trembling and it continues to tremble until God, Lord of Majesty and Perfection, pardons that creature."

Before every act of worship, as prescribed in the Book of God, one should always repent and ask forgiveness of God, Exalted is He. This is the remedy for sin and disobedience: Crush the leaf of repentance and the root of the prayer-for-forgiveness with the pestle of the Affirmation of Unity in the mortar of the heart; moisten with tears, cook in the fire of love, and eat with the spoon of contentment. People of profound understanding have tried this recipe and achieved excellent results.

Those who wish to follow this way must seek only the Essence of the Creator and desire only the Divine Pleasure. They must not remain attached to anything material or spiritual, to their inner states, experiences, and revelations, to sainthood and charismatic powers, but must seek Almighty God with perfect uprightness and sincerity. They must have no goal or desire apart from God, Exalted is He, praying: "My God, You are my goal. All I desire is Your divine pleasure." This abnegation is one of the marks of love and the lover.

The lover should regard every breath he takes as his last, and remember his Lord at every breath. He should look upon each prayer he performs as his last in this life, every session of Remembrance he attends as being his last. He should never for one instant abandon or neglect the Remembrance of God, but must be ever ready and prepared for death, constant in Remembrance, steadfast in prayer, immune from heedlessness.

He should contemplate the bad end he would come to if—God forbid—he should ever be heedless of Remembrance and if at that moment his spirit should leave his body. He must therefore be extremely meticulous and attentive in this respect.

Lovers should eat little and only food that is lawful. It is preferable for them to eat vegetables rather than meat. They should not forget that they are in the Divine Presence even while they lie asleep, so they must never sleep with their legs rudely stretched.

O lover!

Sleep but little. You will soon lie down to a long, long sleep, the morrow of which will be the Day of Resurrection.

It is easy to know God, Glorified and Exalted is He. But to find the way to Him is painfully hard. You cannot find Him without passing beyond your own being. A Sufi does not become a Sufi by sitting on the prayer mat. The dervish way is not just the donning of crown and cloak. A Sufi means one who annihilates himself in the Truth, one whose heart is purified. The Sufi is someone who needs neither the sun by day nor the moon by night. For the Sufi is one who walks night and day by the Light of Truth. Sufism is poverty that can dispense with property. How is one to know one's degree of saintliness and vigilance? Only if all parts of one's body join in the Remembrance of God, Exalted is He, can one be aware of such things. This is the kind of person who is called a Sufi. A Sufi is that mature being who, through his own Remembrance, can hear the praises of all creatures and the Remembrance of the Universe. *Sufi* means one whose heart is *safi,* purified of "all but."

Veracity is saying what is in your heart; sincerity is doing good works for the sake of God alone. To do good works for attention, popularity, and applause is to banish sincerity and bring in hypocrisy. Those whose actions are only for show are called hypocrites.

Say: LA ILAHA ILLA-LLAH MUHAMMADUN RASULU-LLAH at every moment! But do not be content to pronounce this blessed and saving sentence with your tongue alone! Just as you can only declare the Divine Unity with your heart, when you have plunged your head into the pool or into the sea, keep up the affirmation outwardly and inwardly at every moment. Then the gates of revelations may be opened to you, the veils of heedlessness torn aside; you may attain your goal and desire, you may see the Everlasting Beauty. Let your outer be with people, your inner with the Truth. The name dervish is given to those fortunate and blessed people who believe in God and His Messenger, who affirm their faith with their tongues and confirm it with their hearts, who lovingly worship their Lord in abstinence, contentment, and fearful devotion, and who attain the degree of perfection in love and affection for God and His Messenger.

Dervishes keep their beliefs correct in accordance with the doctrines of the People of the Sunna and of the Community. They are faithfully and strictly obedient to the commands of God, Exalted is He. They shun and avoid what God has forbidden. They are extremely wary of heretical innovations, turn away from things that are disapproved of, try not to avail themselves of dispensations but rather to follow the strictest rule. They are resolute in all their actions. In their friendly relations with both their co-religionists and mankind at large they show affection and mercy to all for the sake of God, paying universal regard to the rights of others. They are directed entirely toward God, Exalted is He, and put all their reliance and trust in Him. They are always occupied with Divine Remembrance. Following the laudable precedent of the Chief of Mankind, they keep themselves inwardly and outwardly in a state of ablution. They are extremely wary of empty, unnecessary, and unprofitable talk and conversation, especially backbiting, calumny, cursing, and abuse. They avoid covetousness and harsh words. As well as performing the five daily prayers at the set times, they also observe, as far as possible, the non-compulsory prayers of *ishraq* (shortly after sunrise), *duha* (forenoon), *awwabin* (penitential early evening prayer), and *tahajjud* (during the night). Thus they enliven their nights with ritual prayers. They are never heedless of being in the presence of God, turn away from all that is not He, devote themselves to His service, preserve their integrity, and implore the aid of the spirits of God's saints.

It is possible to cleanse the heart of all but God, to purify the heart of all the dirt and pollution that assail it, by contemplating the Might and Power of God, Exalted is He, and by illuminating the heart with the radiance of God's love and affection and the affection of His Messenger. That heart can thus become the Place of Divine Vision. God's beloved Prophet said:

"Almighty God does not look at your outer form, your lineage and your wealth. He looks into your heart, your intention, and your deeds."

Therefore our hands should be in our work and our hearts with the Beloved.

O seeker of the Truth!

Know this and know it well: A servant's success in worship and obedience to the Truth and in being able to discharge the duties of service, all this depends on the generosity, bounty, and favor of God, Exalted and Sanctified is He. Whatever partial will the creature seems to possess, what effect can the part have on the whole? In other words, what influence can our partial will have on the Divine Will?

So it is with Divine Affection also. It is only when God, Exalted is He, grants His affection to His creature that the creature can have affection for His Lord. Unless God, Glorified and Exalted is He, grants the possibility, unless He considers His affection appropriate to His creature, the creature can neither love nor worship God. Therefore the ability to love his Lord is a very great and high degree for any creature. The more this affection grows, the higher he ascends in spiritual rank. When the servant loves his Lord, he receives an even greater reward for his worship and obedience. When a creature loves God, Exalted is He, it means that God, Magnified and Glorified is He, has considered him fit for His love. It is therefore certain that the Truth loves that creature too and will surely bestow upon him the Paradise of His Essence.

God, Lord of Majesty and Perfection, will resurrect those who love His Essence of Oneness together with those who love God, Exalted is He. At the head of those who love the Truth truly and fittingly come the mighty Prophets and the noble saints. Therefore the Truth, Exalted is He, will gather whoever loves the Prophets and saints together with those they love, both in this world and in the Eternal. In a noble Hadith the Greatest Messenger and revered Prophet said:

"He who loves my example surely loves me, and those who love me are together with me in Paradise."

The conduct that brings a servant close to the Truth, Exalted and Sanctified is He, is loving obedience to the commands of Almighty God, avoidance from fear of God of things disliked by Him, and faithful adherence, with complete dedication and sincerity, to the laudable example of God's beloved Messenger.

If a genuine lover loves another person with a love complete and perfect, he is ready and prepared to sacrifice his all, regardless of profit or loss, for love of that person. For instance, if his loved one invites him to a dangerous place, the lover answers the call wholeheartedly, without pausing to think over what he may be getting himself into. Since common sense and logic always look for the advantage, the lover can also act reasonably and logically for the sake of his beloved. For he is committed to total sacrifice for the loved one's sake.

Just as faith is described in terms of three aspects, so love may be given a three-part interpretation: Hear, see, taste.

These are the stages of faith and love. The genuine lover proves his love with these three conditions. The true believer declares his faith by reaching these three stages, by attaining these three degrees.

Although he has merely heard of love, one who has never been able to experience it still thinks himself a lover. But one without knowledge of love, though imagining himself a lover, would consider it unreasonable and illogical to go somewhere very dangerous in answer to his loved one's call. For he is not a real lover. The real lover also possesses his share of common sense and logic, yet he sacrifices these for love's sake and goes wherever the beloved calls. For the real lover the greatest blessing would be to lay down his very life if need be for his loved one's sake. Such a blessing defies description in speech or writing. It cannot be expressed in words; only lovers who *are* lovers know what this is about. In these matters those who are not real lovers are blind, deaf, and mute. What does the blind know of color, or the deaf of music? How can the mute speak of his condition?

We have been trying to explain things on the material plane. But love is spiritual. Very few are able to grasp spiritual secrets by way of the material, for this is possible only through Divine Grace and the Guidance of the All-Glorious.

If those who love Almighty God with a perfect love will follow His noble Messenger, then He will love them, as He tells us plainly in His Mighty Proof, the Koran, in the noble verses 31-32 of the glorious Sura *al-Imran*.

Following the most noble Messenger, God bless him and give him peace, leads one first to the Sacred Law, then to the Mystic Path, then to Reality, and finally to Inner Knowledge. In other words, the Sacred Law is the gateway to the Unveiling of Love. A house is only entered by its door. The Mystic Path corresponds to the rooms in that house, Reality to a chest kept there, and Inner Knowledge to jewels hidden in that chest. Without entering the house, one cannot enter the room. Without entering the room, one cannot find the chest. Without finding the chest, one cannot take those jewels. Of course, the owner of that house is capable of giving some of those jewels to someone who has entered neither his house nor his room and who does not know the whereabouts of the chest and its contents. It is well known, however, that very few achieve their object in this manner. They are known only to the true owner of all property, that is, God, Glorified and Exalted is He. God's custom has always been and always will be so. The duty incumbent upon the mature individual who ventures upon the path of love is to make every endeavor and to be sure of foot.

I leave it to your wisdom and perceptivity to assess the degree of sincerity in the love of one who protests to his beloved with objections like: "I do love you, but the services and duties you set me and require me to carry out on this path are too heavy for me and I cannot do them. You load me with burdens that are too heavy."

Suppose your beloved says to you: "Open the door of the house and come inside. Come to my room and find me. Be united with me!" If you reply: "I cannot come in through that door, I cannot come up to your room. That is all too much bother and trouble for me," you will surely get this back: "There is no other way it can be done. If it is hard for you to enter my door and too difficult for you to come up to my room, then you will never find me or achieve union with me!"

If you are a real and genuine lover, you must be accustomed to doing your utmost to fulfill the orders of your beloved, even at the risk of your life. Of course, it is just possible that your beloved may deign to come to you.

As we have said, the Sacred Law is the word of the Messenger of Messengers, while the Mystic Path is the acts of God's beloved Prophet. Therefore how can one who does not heed the word of God's Messenger, God bless him and give him peace, does not perform his acts and deeds, does not experience his ecstatic state through knowledge of Reality, how can such a one approach the mysteries that are the Inner Knowledge of the Messenger? Can it be possible for those who do not observe the words, deeds, and state of the Prince of both worlds, by acting in accordance with the Sacred Law, to be able to attain to his secret? Everything is by stage and degree. Every building has a foundation, and even the tallest ladder has a bottom rung.

The same principle applies in both the material and the spiritual sphere. You cannot go on to high school, let alone university, without finishing primary and middle school. Even if you did so, you would not be able to benefit. For, not understanding what you were studying and being taught, you would just be wasting your precious life. A person needs to know where he is coming from and where he is going, why he is coming and why he is going. He should understand the reason for his existence. To know the meaning of life is to grasp the secret of *"Man 'arafa . . ."* ("He who knows [himself, knows his Lord]"). To be the servant of the Truth is to rule the two worlds. To be accepted in the presence of the Truth is possible through serving the Truth truly. God, Exalted is He, loves those who serve his Divine Essence. God, Magnified and Glorified is He, created man, that is Adam and his offspring, the Angels, the jinn, and all other creatures, to know and serve his Divine Essence.

> They reached the Truth because the Truth they served;
> They serve, who have this secret of the Truth observed.

Service begins with faith and belief, love and affection. The starting point or foundation of religious faith is the Sacred Law. Its ceiling is Reality, its content Inner Knowledge. A building without foundations, walls, and roof cannot be. The sovereign will not come to such ruin.

A heart without love is the house of Satan. The Truth will not visit a faithless heart. To deserve a royal visit, a house must be well kept. To be fit for the King of kings, the house must be adorned with faith, love, and affection, and be made spotless. Therefore the task must be started with perfect sincerity and with the Sacred Law; the house of the heart must be tidied and decorated with the Mystic Path; Reality must be reached and Inner Knowledge attained; then with that Inner Knowledge on to Centrality and Proximity . . . . Those who achieve Centrality are steadfast in Devoted Service. This station is the station of Muhammad, vicegerency for God, Exalted is He, as the Perfect Man. It is to be a mirror to the Truth. The station of Muhammad is that of devoted service to God, Glorified and Exalted is He. This is why, in the Testimony of Belief, the noble Prophet's attribute of Servanthood is mentioned before his Messengership (". . . and I testify that Muhammad is His servant and His Messenger").

However, we should not make the vain attempt to compare our condition as servants to that of God's beloved Prophet. For if the service of all creatures were placed in one scale of a balance, and that of God's beloved Messenger in the other, the scale of the Chosen Messenger would surely weigh heavier.

The beginning of service to God is the Affirmation of His Unity, and its end is the same. Its outer and its inner likewise are *Tawhid* (Unity).

Make your heart a Paradise with the garden of *Tawhid,*
Make your mind fragrant with the perfume of *Tawhid.*

Endless journeys to the Kaaba, radiant in black,
Are made by those in love, with one glance of *Tawhid.*

However your face has been sullied by sin,
It will shine clear again with the luster of *Tawhid.*

He rose to the Throne, saw past man's world and jinn's,
Who made the Ascent with the rapture of *Tawhid.*

Veils eighteen thousand with one flash of *Tawhid,*
O Niyazi, from the heart God's intimates have stripped.

10

A PRAYER

Mercy, my God! Mercy, O Pardoner! From us offense, from You munificence. We have come to Your door, O munificent Lord! Our hearts are foul and full of the filth of this world and the grim misfortune of "all but (God)", when those hearts are rightly the place of Divine Vision. Illumine them with the radiance of God's love and affection and the affection of the Messenger of God, in honor of Your beloved Muhammad, the Arabian, his family, his wives, his companions, his helpers, his friends, and his saints, and for the sake of Hasan and Hussein, the pair most comely. Give those hearts joy through the secrets of the Koran's Mighty Proof, and make them conscious through the gracious manifestation of Your beauty. Give us refuge among the special creatures who have attained Your love, ardor, and bliss. Let us quench our thirst with the pure wine of love from the most luminous hands of the Prophet, the Chosen, from 'Ali, the Approved, cup-bearer of Kawthar in Paradise, and from the blessed hands of Hasan and Hussein, the pair most comely. Let us drink our fill, let us pass beyond body and soul with the love of God, let us try on the raiment of Paradise, let us take the path of love, my God! We are disobedient, sinful and wrongdoing creatures. Join us, O Lord, to the caravan of faithful lovers who truly love Your

Divine Essence and the light of Prophethood of Your beloved Messenger, and whose eyes are wet and whose hearts are burned with that love. Include us among those servants You have granted the honor and privilege of being grouped with the saved, for the sake of the pure and innocent blood of Imam Hussein and the martyrs of Karbala', O my Lord! You are Merciful, You are Munificent, You are the Most Generous of the generous, You are the Most Merciful of the merciful, O my God, You are Forgiving and love to forgive, You are Gracious and graciousness is peculiar to You. Confessing our faults, we have come to Your door, we have sought refuge in the gate of Your graciousness. You do not reject the prayer and plea for mercy of sinners who come to Your door, You do not turn away empty-handed those who beg for Pity. Gladden us with Your pardon, make us prosper through Your gracious generosity, record our names among the special servants whom You love, help us in all our difficulties, and increase our blessings both material and spiritual, O my Lord!

Have pity, O intercessor for sinners, O Messenger of God! We are sinners and you are our only intercessor. Intercede for us. We know and believe that your intercession is accepted by God and never rejected; by God, it will not be rejected. Help, O Messenger of God! Pity, O family of the Chosen Prophet! You are the source of generosity and pure mercy. We shelter in your solicitude and compassion and we take refuge in your kindness and sympathy. Yes, we are guilty, wretched, friendless orphans. You are the someone of those who have no one. My compassionate master, my generous king, you are the companion of strangers, the intercessor for the guilty. Do not grudge us your compassion, miserable slaves of our lower selves and playthings of passion that we are, for God's sake reach out and help us. We have plunged into the sea of rebellion and squandered our precious lives in disobedience and oblivion, leaving ourselves feeble and exhausted today. Confessing our faults and our sins, we have held out our hands for Divine Mercy at the gate of

Muhammad. Putting our sin-stained faces on the prayer mat, with our hearts on fire, sighing and sobbing and in tears, we have come to the place of worship of the Divine Presence.

Please graciously accept our repentance as You accepted the repentance of Adam, on him be peace. We are his offspring and we are the Community of God's beloved Muhammad, the refined. We regret our mistakes and the offenses we have committed. We are hostile to the domineering self, so accept our repentance too, and gladden us with Your pardon and grace, O my Lord! You are the Exalted and Generous God who gladdens those who seek His pardon, liberates from Hell those who ask His forgiveness, and grants the blessed favor of His Paradise and His Beauty. You are the Owner of the realm. In everything You do You are triumphant. In all Your works You are most excellent. O my Lord, Highest of the high, my God, the only real object of worship and the True Beloved! There is none worthy of worship and service but You. You alone *are.* You are One. You can have no partner or equal. If You will, You rend and burn. If You will, You cause to prosper and flourish. Only You have the last word on everything, with the command BE. You are the object of our worship, our goal and our desire. If You will, You punish; if You will, You pardon. If You are going to punish, we are Your poor helpless servants. If You pardon, You are the Most Merciful of the merciful. So great is Your Mercy that You grant the right to live even to the unbelievers who deny You. Although they deny You, You do not deprive them of sustenance and You let them benefit from Your blessings. It is You Who give the hypocrites what they want, and satisfy the wishes of the unbelievers. You surely would not deprive and turn away empty-handed from the door of Your Mercy those who affirm Your Unity, who give their hearts to You. So now we too have come to the gate of Your Mercy and held out our hands for Your kindness. Do not turn us away empty-handed, O my Lord! We poor mortal creatures do not refuse those who come to our door, but offer them what You have bestowed upon us. It cannot be, no, it can never be, that You would turn away those who came and sought from You, sad and in despair. Have pity, All-Glorious One, have pity, my King, my God Whom I worship! My exalted Master, my Lord, my God! Our faces and hearts are filthy with sin and rebellion, but let us not be lost on Judgment Day, for we have come to the great Veiler of sins. Fill me with Your love, turn my tears to smiles, make my heart burn with longing for You. My sole ambition and hope is union with You, my God! Just as You rescued Noah, on him be peace, along with those who believed in him, from drowning in the flood, save us also, aboard Your religion which is like Noah's Ark, from getting lost and drowning in the sea of unbelief, the ocean of disobedience and sin. Accord us the joy and delight of faith, the blissful taste of worship, the crown and good fortune of affection, the sovereignty of love. Let us become Your worthy servants in both worlds, and a Community worthy of God's beloved Messenger. Let us follow the example of the Prophet's Sunna. Let us stay firm upon the Straight Path. Let me be extinguished in Your Essence and stay eternally at Your Divine Court. By joining the company of lovers may I be blessed with life everlasting and eternal, O my Lord!

My God, You conferred ten special favors on ten of Your Prophets. As you accepted the repentance of Adam and David, on them both be peace, accept ours also and include us in the company of the penitents. Just as You raised up ldris, peace be upon him, to heaven and let him enter Paradise, so cleanse us of the filth and dirt of this world and elevate us. Let us be characterized by the morality of Islam and of Muhammad, which have the nature of Paradise. Include us among those who enter Paradise in this world by wearing the crown of good conduct, clothing the heart in the light of faith and donning the garment of the Sacred Law, taking heed with the eyes, being attentive with the ears, using the tongue for Remembrance, affirmation of the Divine Unity, and expressions of praise, keeping the feet firmly turned to goodness, being generous with the hands and using them to do good deeds, but leaving the heart with the Beloved, conversant with God, going to meet God, dying before they die and by this death becoming lovers, O my Lord!

As You addressed Moses, on him be peace, with Your mighty speech, send inspiration to our hearts. Let us converse with Your Divine Essence on our Mount Sinai. Let us be among Your special servants who attain the Spiritual Taste, O my Lord!

O my Lord, as You rescued Your faithful friend Abraham from Nimrod's furnace, save us from the fire of our sinister lower selves and do not leave us on our own with them for one moment. O my Lord, protect us against the devil of the self and change the fire of our flesh into light. As You elevated Abraham, on him be peace, to Intimate Friendship, record our names in the register of lovers and introduce us bodily into the company of those You love, O my Lord!

O my Lord, as You recovered Job, on him be peace, from all his sufferings and woes, save us also from the fears and anxieties, sorrows and griefs of this world and the Next, and lead us to comfort and felicity.

O my Lord, as You freed Jonah, on him be peace, from the belly of the fish, set us free also from the hand of the foe, the tyranny of ignorance, and the calamity of unbelief, and bring us to safety.

As You restored his kingdom to Solomon, on him be peace, make us as pure as on the day we were born and gratify us with material property and spiritual fortune, O my Lord!

As You raised Imam Hussein, may God be pleased with him, to the rank of martyrdom, let us live auspiciously and obtain the intercession of all the martyrs, O my Lord! For the sake of the martyrs' blessed blood, shield us from corrupt belief, help us to achieve Your noble pleasure, and make us true believers who attain a perfection and completeness of faith conforming to the faith of Your beloved Messenger, O my Lord!

Let our last words be the affirmation of Divine Unity and the Glorious Koran, O my Lord, while our tongues utter Remembrance and declare the Divine Unity, and while our eyes behold Paradise and Your Beauty, manifest Your Essence as You include us in the fellowship of Your special servants to whom You address the glorious command:

"O self secure in faith, you with your Lord and He with you contented, return to meet your Lord, enter among My special servants, enter with them My own Paradise" (Koran 89:27-30).

Join us, O my Lord, with those blessed and happy beings who pass from Your Majesty to reach Your Beauty, who are granted Your pardon from Your justice, who enter Paradise by Your grace, who behold the beauty of the Chosen Prophet, who are put to dwell in Paradise on high near to Your refined Beloved and who attain the Everlasting Beauty of Your face!

O Conqueror unconquerable! Make our state endure with justice, grant our forces the secret of *wa-yansuraka'-llahu nasran 'aziza* "May God grant you a mighty victory" (Koran 48:3). Make glorious in both worlds those who serve religion and state, and especially this peculiar and honorable nation, with justice and equity for the Truth's sake. Assemble us beneath the flag of 'Umar ibn al-Khattab, may God be pleased with him, and resurrect us under the banner of glory. Exalt the degrees of the martyrs and the ranks of the champion warriors. O my Lord, assemble our lawfully earning merchants under the flag of Abu Bakr the Veracious, may God be pleased with him; the servants of learning, Koran, religion, faith, and the believers, under the banner of 'Uthman ibn 'Affan, may God be pleased with him; the manly heroes who set an example to all humanity by putting their knowledge into practice by their perfect tolerance, patience and endurance, boldness and courage, zeal and munificence, generosity and virtue—under the flag of Imam 'Ali, may God ennoble his countenance and be pleased with him. O my Lord, resurrect those who are wronged together with Imam Hasan the Chosen, and the martyrs wrongfully slain together with Imam Hussein, the victim of Karbala' (may God be pleased with them all). O my Lord, assemble under the banner of the Lion of God's Messenger, Hamza, may God be pleased with him, those who fall as martyrs at sea, on land, and in the air for the sake of God, to exalt the Word of God, for the ideal of humanity, for freedom and independence, for motherland and nation, to guard their honor, chastity, and good name, for the sake of all that is sacred! For the sake of the eye that weeps for fear of God, for the sake of the heart that burns with the love of God, for the sake of the word spoken in the name of God, for the sake of Torah, Gospel, Psalms, and illustrious Koran, for the sake of creatures who never for a moment forget but always remember Your Divine Essence, for the sake of Uways al-Qarani and all the great founding saints, for the sake of the lovers, the truthful, the sincere, the devoted, and the pious, for the sake of the doctrine of Abu Hanifa al-Nu'man, for the sake of the beauty of the face of Joseph of Canaan, graciously deign to accept these prayers and supplications, O my Lord!

O my Lord, forgive those who remember in their prayers this poor, humble servant of Yours, Muzaffer Ashki, forgive them in both worlds for the sake of Your refined and beloved Prophet, and may those who recite one noble Fatiha for me after my death be immersed in the Fatiha when they come to die!

My God, bestow Your blessing on Your refined and beloved Prophet, his family, his children, his wives, his helpers, his companions, and his friends, especially his upright Caliphs Abu Bakr, 'Umar, 'Uthman, and 'Ali, upon them all be the pleasure of God, Exalted is He, together with all who love them till the Day of Resurrection and Judgment! Let Your guidance escort us. Cause this little book of ours to be read. Enlighten inwardly and outwardly with the Light Divine all those who read it or listen to it read aloud. Gladden them all with Your grace and guidance, afford them Your direction, enable them to breathe their last as true believers, O my Lord! May this humble work of ours find acceptance and approval and be pleasing in the sight of God and His noble Messenger. Make the lovers who read it worthy of Your love. Make us happy by accepting our supplications, O my Lord!

Subhana Rabbika Rabbi-l-'izzati 'amma yasifun wa-salamun 'ala-l-mursalin wa-l-hamdu lillahi Rabbi-l-'alamin. Al-Fatiha . . .

(Glory to your Lord, the Lord of Might, beyond all they describe. And peace upon the Messengers and thankful praise to the Lord of the Worlds. Let us recite the Fatiha . . . .)

The Loved One within makes the lover's life thrive;
The veil of Self-Knowledge he finds his way past.
In Unity's circle, if he's all alive,
His drop becomes sea, then he finds Ocean vast.

Who drinks love's goblet from the perfect guide
Straightway finds himself the beloved beside;
Comes love, and the lover's will is set aside,
Then, bidden "Return!" he finds his Lord at last.

This transient world's basis and frame is love;
Here and Hereafter the lover's aim is love;
He serves, obeys, and works to proclaim his love;
Who lives with love, to Paradise comes at last.

From East to West, whichever the way you go,
That lovers are legion experience will show;
For man in our age is longing Truth to know,
In the depths of his heart he'll find it at last.

Calling ILLA-LLAH the spheres are gyrating,
Calling ILLA-LLAH the Angels rotating,

A PRAYER

Calling ILLA-LLAH the hearts are vibrating,
The cure for his pain must each one find at last.

On love's rough path the way is easily lost;
The way to union is not so quickly crossed.
This secret can be known but not without cost;
The genuine lover finds God's grace at last.

It seems to poor Ashki he's by the world pressed,
He comes to the Palace of Union a guest,
In trouble he is by the master addressed,
Finds Nureddin Jerrahi, Sultan, at last.

APPENDIX

Official Rulings on The Sufi Practice of Whirling

Watching the lovers whirling in worship as they remember and proclaim the Divine Unity, certain unperceptive onlookers may reach the conclusion that the dervishes are merely playing games or dancing. But it is known and accepted by men of real understanding that a grave sin is incurred by comparing the Remembrance of God to a game or dance, or by jumping to such superficial conclusions. To compare the Remembrance of God, and the whirling movements associated with it, to mere play-acting is an error as serious and unpardonable as equating lawful sex with adultery and fornication, or military service with murder. For while it is true that there is a similarity in each case from the point of view of the action, in meaning and nature they are utterly different and distinct. To pretend otherwise is certainly to invite the displeasure of God, Exalted is He.

Sheikh al-Islam and
Grand Mufti Ebu-Su'ud

The following are two of three rulings issued by Zenbilli Ali Efendi on the subject of Sufi whirling. Those who wish to see the third may look it up in the book containing the collected rulings of Jemali

Efendi, God's Mercy upon him. They should also refer to *Fetavay-i Omeriyye* (The Rulings of 'Umar).

1

Question: If members of a Sufi society, meeting to remember God, should stand up and perform their Remembrance while turning around and around, and if they fervently call out *ALLAH . . . HU,* is the way these people perform their Remembrance lawful or unlawful? If you declare it lawful, are those who call them unbelievers to be regarded as unbelievers themselves? May you be rewarded for the favor of a clarification.

Response: God knows best. Whatever their mode of Remembrance, the Sufis are not unbelievers. Perhaps those who call them unbelievers are unbelievers themselves.

2

Question: If members of a Sufi society whirl in their Circle of Remembrance and perform their Remembrance while turning around and around, and if X should say: "The members of this Circle of Remembrance, those who conduct the turning and those who declare it lawful, are unbelievers," how does X stand under Islamic law? Clarification is requested.

Response: God, Exalted is He, knows best. To be convinced of the truth of this stricture constitutes unbelief. To be readmitted to Islam, X would have to renew his declaration of faith and recontract his marriage [annulled by his unbelief]. The magistrates of Islam must administer severe chastisement to those who slander the Sufis in this manner.

Signed: Ali Jemali, may God pardon him

Here are a few more examples of the noble rulings on whirling and Remembrance of God performed in a standing position, given by holders of the office of Sheikh al-Islam whose blessed names are engraved in the annals of history and in human memory.

1

Question: Is it correct to say that the members of that noble fraternity, in considering it lawful to perform their rituals of Remembrance audibly, are in conformity with the Divine Law and are following their path in felicity and right belief, in accordance with statements by the two honorable Imams declaring such practices permissible? (What is referred to here is not the form of whirling which is prohibited.) O God, show the truth truly.

Response: Whoever believes those Muslims to be unbelievers is himself an unbeliever. If he abuses them, he is to be chastised. Such is the response of the Hanafi Imams in clarification of this problem.

Question: Suppose X were to say to some people gathered in a certain place for whirling in accordance with the Sacred Law: "Whirling is an invention of the Samaritans; to remember God in this way is unlawful; if you consider it worship you are unbelievers, should you die in this condition you are not to be washed or prayed over and may not be buried in Muslim cemeteries." What is the legal situation of X?

Response: God knows best whether this is dancing. The Imams of the faith have given seventy definitions of dance. Dancing is separate. What happens in the Circle of Remembrance is not dancing.

Signed: Valizade, Sheikh al-Islam

APPENDIX

2

Question: (From Sultan Mehmed IV): What is the response of the Hanafi Imams in clarification of the following problem? If those people believe it an act of worship to make Remembrance in accordance with the Divine Law, and if they perform the ritual of whirling in Remembrance of God, should anything be done about those people for performing their whirling? May you be rewarded for your explanation.

Response: God knows best, but I have no doubt that audible Remembrance of God was considered permissible by the Imams of the faith, especially the two honorable Imams, and that they rose to the highest ranks and discovered the glorious miracles. It is therefore my noble verdict that in this matter the honored doctrine and illustrious rulings of the two Imams be put into effect forthwith by mighty decree. Furthermore, the disbelievers should not be allowed to interfere with the aforementioned Sheikh. Stubborn recalcitrants should be imprisoned for long terms until they exhibit unmistakable penitence. Let them be subject to all kinds of forced labor and correction, and be obliged to renew their declaration of faith in Islam and recontract their marriages, unless they submit to the noble Sacred Law and give credence to the aforementioned Sheikh. Let this be a salutary lesson to others and a cause of benefits. Let this imperial judgment be recorded in the protected register, let its contents always be complied with, and let it remain in the possession of the aforementioned Sheikh so that he may rely upon the noble emblem. [Written at the beginning of the month of Sha'ban, A.H. 1077, in the city of Constantinople.]

3

Question: (from the Sheikh al-Islam Muhammad Sa'duddin Efendi): What is the response of the Hanafi Imams to the following: Suppose an assembled congregation stand up while making Remembrance; is it permissible if they turn around and around voluntarily, i.e., of their own volition? May you be rewarded for the favor of a clarification.

Response: It is permissible; it is valid; there is no restriction upon the Remembrance of God.

Signed: Efdal Zade

4

Question: What is the response of the Hanafi Imams concerning the following problem? Suppose a group of poor monotheists stand up while performing Remembrance of God and, while remembering God, Exalted is He, sometimes chant divine words containing wise advice, sometimes weep and sometimes groan—if they proclaim the Divine Unity while turning around and around in accordance with the Koranic injunction "Remember God standing, sitting, and on your sides" (Koran 4:103), what does this entail in Sacred Law? May you be rewarded for the favor of an explanation.

Response: Abundant blessings are entailed.

Signed: Ebu-Su'ud

5

Question: What is the response of the Hanafi Imams concerning the following problem? Suppose poor monotheists gather in small mosques, the great congregational mosques, and other noble places, perform Remembrance of God while sitting, standing, and perhaps revolving, and say that Remembrance of God is an act of worship and that whirling is a lawful form of movement. If a set of ignoramuses should accuse them of unbelief, thinking that they hope to cheat death by means of their Remembrance of God, and if they should say that they would not follow them as prayer-leaders or exchange greetings with them—what is the position in Sacred Law of a mob who talk like that? May you be rewarded for the favor of an explanation.

Response: God knows best, but there is no disputing the fact that the aforementioned poor monotheists are perfect believers. Perhaps countless and innumerable saints of God will appear among them. As for those ignorant sermonizers who accuse them of disbelief—God forbid!—in the appointed hour of death, because they perform Remembrance of God and believe its movements and motions to be lawful, they fall into their own pit in keeping with the saying "He who digs his brother's well falls into it." If they persist in their mistaken notion, it will not be permissible to follow them in prayer, and if they do not repent and renew their profession of faith, it becomes necessary to cut off exchange of greetings and conversation with them and to treat them in all respects as unbelievers.

Signed: Ebu-Su'ud, Sheikh al-Islam

INDEX